The Power of Emptiness

Being, Knowing, and Not Doing

Lujan Matus

Disclaimer

All rights reserved. No part of this publication may be reproduced or transferred in any form or by any means, graphic, electronic, or mechanical, including photocopying, recording, taping, or by any information storage retrieval system, without the written permission of the author. The author specifically disclaims any responsibility for any liability, loss, or risk, personal or otherwise, which is incurred as a consequence, directly or indirectly, of the use and application of any of the contents of this book.

© Copyright 2021 Lujan Matus.
The Parallel Perception logo is copyright.
No unauthorized use.
ISBN-10: 8589796223
ISBN-13: 979-8589796223

www.parallelperception.com

Acknowledgements

To Mizpah Matus, Elizabeth Aires, Rakel Stephanian, Kory Matthew and Maka Shen.

Thank you all for your loving time and diligent efforts towards the proof-reading process. I appreciate you so much.

Naomi Jean, thank you for your time and efforts in formatting, cover artwork and design, and the back of the book description.

www.parallelperception.com

SPECIAL THANKS

To Naomi, my dearest, most loving companion.
Thank you from the depth of my heart for being once again involved in the production of this book. Your editorial alterations are always superb. You have enhanced my journey.

To you, Janina, thank you for your phenomenal love and devotion in helping me to bring this book to fruition within a ten-week period. You are just amazing.

Thank you to Elizabeth for your generosity.
You are a beautiful being.

To the love of my life, Mizpah. I adore you.

www.parallelperception.com

TABLE OF CONTENTS

ACKNOWLEDGEMENTS .... ♥

SPECIAL THANKS .... ♥

FOREWORD I

INTRODUCTION VIII

DEDICATION XII

PREFACE XIII

THE MANGO GROVE MASTER 1

THE IMMATURE SEED 18

PATIENTLY WAITING 29

ABUNDANCE 35

I AM A MOUNTAIN, I AM 43

MY TEACHER 57

www.parallelperception.com

PATHWAYS OF MY MEMORY 62

THE SHEPHERD..78

THE MOUNTAIN..88

THE BODHI TREE 106

THE RIDDLE...113

MORPHOGENESIS...126

MISPLACED MEMORIES PART ONE 148

MISPLACED MEMORIES PART TWO 159

THE UNDOING 174

BE IN THE WORLD BUT NOT OF IT 183

THE PASSERBY...194

HEAVEN AND EARTH 206

THE POWER OF THE OLD TIBETAN........228

THE CHANT 246

AS I AM..255

THE BLESSING 266

GRATITUDE 296

www.parallelperception.com

Foreword

This story begins with Lujan asking me one day to become involved in transcribing and editing his new book, *The Power of Emptiness*.

My heart exploded with gratitude and excitement, for I knew I would be taking a deep dive into the *Unknown*.

Oh, boy! It's ten weeks since we began, and this has been a journey that's one of a kind.

Even though English is not my first language and I had no idea what book writing entailed, having studied with Lujan for years and after talking to him about my insecurities, he helped me realize that my perceived disadvantage was not an obstacle. I knew enough to be able to take notes. What I had no clue about was how this process would transform me.

To put this simply, it has been the most amazing, intense, and equally rewarding time of my life. I am forever grateful to my loving Teacher, Lujan Matus, for giving me this opportunity and patiently guiding me on my path.

This book is a process that reveals, in a straightforward way, his fundamental teachings. It showed me what I needed to do and not do next on my journey. Step by step, like an upward spiral, each chapter illuminated aspects of my consciousness I was not aware of, clearing the doubts that cloaked my sacred heart.

As I witnessed my deepest weeds being gently uprooted, I realized this process could become an overwhelming experience in the absence of the sincere approach, steadfast determination, and compassion of a loving teacher. Those of you who have taken classes with Lujan will know of what I speak.

Now, looking back, I only see glimpses of our time

together, laughing for thirty minutes straight, until our faces and bellies ached. Or bursting into tears in complete abandon, filled with gratitude, love, and understanding.

For many, my description may seem unusual as Lujan is a reclusive kind of Teacher. Yet, there's a part of his wonderful being that most would love to meet. He said to me when this process began, "I need to be surrounded by kind and loving people." This simple statement brought tears to my eyes and opened up my heart to recognize such a fundamental truth we all search for in our lives.

It also made me realize something: motive will always stop one from establishing a genuine communion with one's Teacher. Getting close to him but not to one's own heart is a lost opportunity. I now understand why Lujan always says, *Be your simple, loving self*. It is the only way to progress.

This book taught me not to miss the chance to be within my purpose, stay on my path, and accept full responsibility for the results of my life. It also teaches commitment to the present moment as a joyful expression of the heart.

Practicing *Lo Ban Pai*, Lujan's movement system as a physical application to his philosophy, increases fortitude and bestows clarity, strength, and determination. I am lucky to have already studied some of the forms so I could see how our daily interaction reflected back in my practice.

I remember the first workshop I attended, learning the form *Golden Lotus* and my initial encounter with Lujan. My heart recognized immediately that my search for a Teacher had come to an end. There I discovered the most unbiased reflection that a Master can embody for his students, revealing who they really are within that moment of communion.

And even though such an intense gaze as his can sometimes be daunting, years later, after witnessing many of his interactions with his other students, I realized his sharp, powerful focus is exactly what is needed to dispel any disharmonious feelings so that they could come upon their own heart. Not through blame, shame, nor guilt but through their own realizations.

Each story that Lujan, as the Mango Grove Master, so generously imparts to his disciples has the power of his life experience behind it. The way these stories resonated in my own life, as I believe they will resonate within yours, is a still-unfolding revelation.

The events that are presented here are practical examples of how communication actually happens, and I have generously been given the space to ask questions that clarified some of my own curiosities. One of the answers the Master elucidates in the *Heaven and Earth* chapter is in relation to my inquiry about an extraordinary thing I observed during one of the training sessions I participated in.

It was in Langkawi, an island in the Asian Pacific, the second time I was interacting with Lujan. He was teaching us a form called *Opening the Tao* and briefly demonstrating its martial application to one of the students. I still can't reconcile what took place. It seems like a dream to me when I remember how the student gently touched him, only to spring backward quite high up into the air. There was a feeling of shock in my chest when this happened, but I did not understand it nor dare to ask about it.

Looking back on it, Lujan relayed to me he had forgotten I was even there on that day. I suppose one of the reasons why is that I did not find the courage to stand up and inquire, so this greatly diminished our chance to truly meet.

Simultaneously, I recall another instance that I directly experienced inside my body and found surprising. Lujan was teaching us about something pertinent to that moment when he suddenly rose from his chair. My body mimicked his instantaneously, only to find myself wondering why I had stood up as well. After bringing to shelter the clothes that had been hanging outside to dry in the open air, he clarified and said that gentle raindrops had begun to pour. He had stood up quickly, and my body was pulled up by his movement unexpectedly in response.

One of the things that make the *Lo Ban Pai* philosophy so effective is how it teaches one to be completely engaged within the present moment while waiting for the knowledge pertinent to one's path to be revealed out of apparently unimportant or seemingly innocuous experiences.

"It's strange how consciousness works," Lujan said many times, voicing my astonishment at how complex and interrelated everything is. He is also aware that I, like many others, need the correct guidance to navigate these frequencies that become available through diligent practice and sincere application of the principles he imparts.

I believe these timeless teachings, so generously expounded upon here, are essential and practical tools that enable us to take command of our dysfunctional emotions and mind chatter, and subdue them once and for all so that the expression of one's heart may mirror back its untainted reflection, revealing the wisdom hidden within.

JANINA OPREA

Introduction

Scanning the chapter titles for clues on how to introduce this incredible book, I see a treasure trove of perceptual seeds, now alive and fertile in my consciousness, ready to bloom anew within every moment.

To witness the Old Sage guide his young students on their journey of learning how to tend to the precious mango grove is to be introduced to a world of deeply empathic interpersonal conduct. Every heartfelt exchange and the utterly applicable instructions that are seamlessly woven into the fabric of the lives of the Mango Grove Master and his disciples are unforgettable life lessons.

INTRODUCTION

The unfolding metaphors of the saplings and the older trees, the sweet and sour fruit, and all of the crucial elements that make up a lifetime of devotion are luminous with meaning and take on mythic dimensions in terms of how they integrate with one's consciousness.

As the disciples mature, so too does their understanding of the profound wisdom their beloved teacher has to share, including the intricacies and soft power rooted in the application of *Being, Knowing, and Not Doing*. The Old Sage's poignantly conveyed teachings impress upon us pragmatic foundations regarding how to apply oneself, demonstrating the power of uncontrived presence, the true perils of motive, and how our actions really do echo throughout eternity.

Outside the confines of time and beyond the grove we encounter the Master's teacher, the old Tibetan, who introduces us to the Mountain and the vivid lessons of his path. Through the words of these venerable sages we discover the multi-dimensional insights hidden within the many lifetimes they have witnessed.

INTRODUCTION

To recognize oneself within the reflections of their moments is to trace a very personal trail through the deepest recesses of your heart. Revelatory perspectives intertwine with the memories of a lifetime to illuminate new ways of seeing the trials and tribulations one has faced. Possibilities of forgiveness and renewal become internally available through key teachings that provide fluid frameworks through which to witness our ongoing journey.

You will discover the meaning of *Heaven and Earth* as an internal confluence of energies; learn to recognize the *Thief* and the *Ghost;* disengage from the intricacies of the *Curse* to become the *Blessing;* and identify the crucial distinction between the perceptual functions of *Wooden Spokes* and *Holographic Wheels.* What makes these precious truths so vibrant is that they align with what is seen, all around and within, from the broadest overview to the subtlest degree imaginable.

I feel honored to witness the eternal refinement of Lujan's teachings within each moment. I wholeheartedly recommend all of his works, but this one presents the essence of who he is and what he has to share in a very beautiful way. Even after twenty years of being continually blown away by his awe-inspiring wisdom and the abiding consistency of his loving friendship, I am experiencing this book as a series of unexpected revelations.

Lujan's ability to return us home, to our heartfelt origin, is unique. The insights within these pages bring tears of joy and laughter, realization and relief, unlocking, unravelling and equipping me in ways that seem so simple yet are so finely observed and elegantly conveyed that my resistances are humbled into retreat. To put it plainly, it is changing me, and I believe it will change you, too.

The Power of Emptiness will open your eyes and heart in ways that cannot be anticipated. What is shared here will give you back the sovereignty you seek, reinstate the beauty of your moments, beckon the tenderness of your care, and much, much more. This is why we love and cherish Lujan Matus so dearly.

NAOMI JEAN

Dedication

In loving memory of

Wendy Nolin

1972 – 2021

We all love you very much.

PREFACE

In dedication to those who follow my work, I appreciate that you find solace and empowerment within the books that I have written and welcome you with enthusiasm into this new edition.

Over the last two decades an uncalculated coherence has magically revealed itself, page by page, within every book. Essentially, the whole collection serves to illuminate many facets of the wisdom embedded within *Lo Ban Pai*, the encompassing practices and philosophy that I have dedicated my life to transmitting.

PREFACE

The Power of Emptiness is specifically designed to work in concert with *Whisperings of the Dragon* and *Who Am I?* to fortify and expand upon the principles embedded within the system that I teach.

Who Am I? describes the inner workings of my life as an empath, the profound quality of that state, and how every human being on this planet is in possession of this heartfelt potential, hindered only by the socially-engineered conditioning we have all been subjected to.

Whisperings of the Dragon details the preliminary aspects of *Being, Knowing, and Not Doing,* how to attain inner silence, and the dangers of seeking validation. The intent behind these two editions is to enable anyone who is devoted to the transformation of their consciousness to break through the present-day edifice and arrive upon their true nature.

However self-evident these truths are to me, I became aware that there was a need for further clarification. I realized that many of my students were still struggling with life itself and needed guidance on how to navigate the complexities of perception. I believe this eighth publication will endow each one of you with the power to proceed with humble confidence.

Ushering my students into an unimpeded state of empathic communion is the purpose of this book. The basic philosophy of *Lo Ban Pai* is simplicity itself. *To walk the path of life as your beautiful, loving self is all that matters.*

Within this offering, I hope that you will encounter who you are, and define who you are truly meant to become. May that discovery reverberate within your life to touch upon all those you love with utmost tenderness.

I welcome you now into the *Power of Emptiness*.

LUJAN MATUS

Recognize what is before you,

and what is hidden will be revealed;

for there is nothing coveted

that will not be made manifest.

Yeshua

THE MANGO GROVE MASTER

There is a fascinating story that originated in India, where so many people love to consume sweet mangos. I became aware of it ten years ago and realized it would be a great tool for instructing everybody in *the art of Being, Knowing, and Not Doing.*

So here is where I slip behind the scenes as the venerable Master and tell this mysterious tale from my own perspective, thus interlocking the practical applications of internal alchemy within the *Lo Ban Pai* system, which translates as *Elegantly Flourishing Spirals.*

It begins with a wise old sage who tended a lush mango

grove situated a short walk from a village. In the center, there was an ancient Bodhi tree next to a clear pond where unusually large, black and white fish swam joyfully. This attracted many of the villagers who would often come to meditate and sit with the beloved Master and ask questions of him pertaining to his wisdom and their lives.

Because of all of his experience and the beautiful, sweet fruit the mango crop always yielded, he was variously known within the surrounding area as the Master of the Mango Grove, the Grove Master, Master Turya, or simply, the Old Sage.

The villagers noticed that he was quite advanced in years and requested if he could take some of the children from their community as his disciples so that his wisdom may be passed on to the next generation. Master Turya agreed to this and randomly chose nine of them to be admitted into his tutelage, gifting each a small machete to wear on their hip.

The Mango Grove Master commenced the instruction for the young boys on how to look after the entirety of the orchard so that it would stay prosperous and successful, yielding juicy, sweet mangos by showing them the old grove, the Bodhi tree and the fish pond.

"Now that you are in your ninth year of life and ready to move forward with my instructions," the wise sage began, "there are certain things that I will require you all to do, in harmony with one another.

As you know, the grove has been here for many years. It provides delicious, sweet mangos to our village and feeds many, causing great happiness to occur through the consumption of these beautiful fruits upon their ripening.

We have two hundred trees and this established orchard will be tended by you, as you simultaneously care for the nine new saplings that I have prepared."

"Follow me," the Mango Grove Master said lovingly, "to see how I water, fertilize, and nurture the old trees that have been in this grove for longer than your life so that you may adapt to tending to what is there while you are waiting for the saplings to mature."

Master Turya asked the boys to follow him through the

orchard, and what they noticed was how gentle and aware he was of everything that happened around and in between every tree that he cared for.

As he caressed a branch of a deep-rooted mango plant, he said to them, "This old *Being* has ancient wisdom embedded within it. By virtue of its connection to the planet, it represents whom you are going to become. Realize, when you eat its fruit, it becomes you. But can you enter its subtleties through this act of communion? That is the question."

The Grove Master resumed, "The fruit of this *Being*, when digested, brings joy deep inside of your body. Its sweetness, its vibrant color becomes you. Yet when you observe it hanging from the branch, before it enters your body, you don't realize that it's vibrating this way—until you taste it."

Looking at the boys, he softly continued, "Realize that this magnificent *Being* is static. It is less animated than a person. Its stillness is profound."

One of the boys looked up and asked, "Master, what other lessons can it convey to us? Can you tell us?"

The Old Sage smiled and answered, "If you were to take one sapling and walk around with it, disconnected from the ground, our Mother Earth, it would not survive. But if you sit gently and accompany it within its stillness, it can convey to your body how to observe yourself within a profound state of self-reflection that harbors no memories yet has a subtle responsiveness to the world around it, without the quality of its personality becoming involved."

"But Master, what does this really mean?" another disciple insisted.

The kind and patient Old Sage replied, "It teaches us how to be neutral, how to enter the perception of *No Place*, through the phenomena of realizing that the face of *Emptiness* is composed of inward neutrality. From its deep stillness, we cannot see its responsiveness to us. The question is: What has been eliminated within it which renders it absolutely open to everything in its environment?"

The boys seemed perplexed, not really understanding what Master Turya had just said.

"You are a human being," he clarified, looking affectionately down at them. "Your humanness seems easy to understand. It is your *Beingness* that is profound. I will explain the complex interactions between these two qualities to you, in more depth, as time goes by.

Now I must carefully show you the course of action you need to undertake to comprehend my teachings."

"There are many varieties of mango trees, and I have chosen these nine for you to have guardianship of," said the Grove Master, gesturing towards a group of young saplings waiting to be planted. "This species takes seven to eleven years to mature into the stage of bearing fruit, and this will suit the purpose of instructing you in the complexities of the ancient Art of *Being, Knowing, and Not Doing*.

These plants symbolize my wisdom becoming renewed within you. Thus, this oral tradition will survive by you being here, with me. As they gently grow into their maturity, so will you," he explained.

"No more trees will be introduced into the flourishing grove that we are tending until your time under the wings of my tutelage is completed," he continued. "By then, you'll be more than halfway through your life, and everything that I say to you now that you can't yet fully comprehend will be profoundly remembered, in comparison to your own personal realizations."

Master Turya asked the boys to accompany him and proceeded to dig nine holes. After adding composted fertilizer mixed in with dry cow dung, he looked up and mentioned to them, "At this early point of maturation, we must be careful with the fertilization process."

While demonstrating this, the Old Sage completed his explanation, "Too much fertilizer may hurt the tender roots, for it is acidic, and that can burn them. This is similar to your life that you are going to experience with me. I must fertilize your consciousness carefully; otherwise, too much stimuli, in terms of learning too quickly without the time of your life experience to balance all the elements of your comprehension may damage your growth since you are not ready for the complexity of my wisdom yet.

It takes quite a while for these trees to produce their buds. During this time, while you will be attending the old orchard, I want you to stand quietly next to these *Beings* and carefully observe your internal feelings and listening power gradually arising from within.

The specific posture that I will teach you in a minute will allow you to become aware of the vast mycelia network that surrounds the roots of the old trees in the established grove and how it slowly reaches towards the saplings."

He then proceeded to show them how to adjust their head, shoulders, hips, knees, and feet in a specific alignment and instructed them on how to breathe deeply into the lower abdomen and locate its exact center.

"The elbows must be dropped towards the *Earth* so they become anchored to the lower gourd in coordination with a particular way of opening the palms, which possess a command center or chakra," explained the Grove Master.

"You must remember to softly intend upon this area, concentrating your energy into the absolute center of your lower gourd, just like a peacock within its nest, sitting on its egg," Master Turya added, smiling.

"You see how these birds brood so devotedly during this time: They close their eyes and by focusing on their breath like a delicate drum beating its continuous rhythm towards this point, they meditate to tenderly awaken the embryo within its shell. This form of absorption will draw the bird's focus away from the external world, thus concentrating within ninety-eight percent of its eyes and one hundred percent of its listening capacity, in coordination with its feeling of devotion.

This example will help inform your body how to proceed with this *Inaction*, by *Not Doing* what you generally have done all your life up to this point, which is to relentlessly expand your energy beyond its limits by being totally engaged within the process of the world around you.

This is very much like a fox chasing our chickens. They all get startled and upset and run in whichever direction without any focus, compulsively clucking and drawing everybody into their drama," the Grove Master said, trying to contain his laughter.

"You must incrementally withdraw from this process, and this is how your attention will return to its source.

While standing, also concentrate upon the bones inside your body to extend themselves towards *Heaven,* as you feel your flesh being pulled towards *Earth*. This will affect the complex of sinews within your system to transform slowly, over a period of three to five years.

This is one of the pathways that the mycelia complex can travel through in coordination with your lower gourd being sunk to the point that it grabs your soft tissues when it begins to move, activated by other exercises that you will do with the palms of your hands unified with your center.

In the years to come, I will ask you to use your ears and eyes to inwardly listen while traveling through your body to discover where the flesh is held in a state of resistance.

You will learn to release this by recognizing that it is

your mind, not your body, that is, at this point, incapable of letting go of all the nuances that your internal rivers locate within the process of your journey towards the ground.

I will explain to you about this somatic phenomenon called *Rivers of Light* that originate from your upper gourd's primary purpose, which is to watch from within. In other words, the internal eye, accompanied by the listening power of your ears, will learn to flow down through these hallways, through all the tributaries that become available to its perception at any point of location that may be stubbornly held by the mind. Resistance is the first element that must be transformed.

The internal dialogue, with all of its control mechanisms, is a dwarf in stature in comparison to the rivers of the somatic experience that will eventually neutralize the mind's holding patterns and thus command it to flow through the body, stimulating its communion with the *Earth* underneath your feet.

Once the rationale belonging to this cerebral intelligence meet its destination, its influence will begin to dissolve within the power of our magnetic potential that resides within the *Earth*. At this point, your heart will be released from its imprisoned confines and will be capable of expressing its sovereign capacity to speak on behalf of what you see. Your whole *Being* will then learn to listen with the feelings of this centralized gourd within your physical form.

Not only will this occur, but the radiance of your heart-fire will consume all that is not meant to be and transmute it into your capacity to truly see what is surrounding you.

These are some of the internal secrets that the Bodhi tree, which you will become acquainted with in this grove, will transmit to you when you learn to sit in stillness with me. In doing so, you will discover the wondrous effect of all the subtleties that may arise from the methods of breathing that I will reveal to you as the years go by."

"Master, how can we become more familiar with this process inside of our body?" one of the boys inquired.

Turning towards his disciple, the Old Sage replied, "By realizing that your body is being pulled as if it is losing its balance towards the old grove, even though you are static and upright. But at no point should you embellish or imagine that you feel this. It is a very delicate process that first requires many things to stop within your *Being* so you may realize these subtle magnetic phenomena that will seem to appear from without yet animate themselves within you.

It is like being dizzy, the feeling you have when you twirl in circles when you are playing games, and you feel that everything is trying to pull you this way and that. This is the beginning of your body realizing that it can extend itself beyond its physical limits."

The boys were elated by what they were learning and waited excitedly to hear more. "You can also look at it this way," the Master continued. "When you wish to pick up a cup, you lean forward to grasp it. But realize that your mind does not acknowledge that the body started the movement first and takes credit for this occurring, thus obscuring the pre-emptive nature of your physicality.

The mind is small and insignificant. You must take it from your higher center and pop it under your right foot, the same way Shiva did so as to control its impulses, but at no point are we controlling anything. It is what we *Don't Do* that matters," Master Turya revealed.

"As you become accustomed to this phenomenon, the old grove will send its lights to you through this conductive process which will be magnetically transmitted. If you stand still and are patient enough, this will become your electric capacity to communicate with other *Beings* silently and this is the beginning of the *Heavenly* process.

But its manifestation will vary according to your physical configuration, facial features, and general predisposition, including the length and density of your bones in proportion with your whole body. So, what I am saying is everybody is unique, and the destiny of their timeline will adapt to these factors.

The lights received through the center of your feet into your body are there to protect and guide you on your journey of communion with these young saplings, as their caretakers.

This is the beginning of understanding the principle of

Heaven and *Earth*. This is the journey that every disciple must undertake to comprehend their empathic nature.

The exchanges of the mycelial complex are not too dissimilar from an empathic communion between Master and disciple. This is exactly the process of *Earth* beginning to connect with *Heaven*, the *Father of the Sky*.

This is the expression of Shiva's accomplishments, one of the greatest sages that was ever known in India, and this will help you expand into the mysteries of the sinking and rising force of the *Earth* into your body. This is the lesson of internal alchemy that he endeavored to impart during his lifetime.

The circle that surrounds his statue, in actuality, is a wheel that has flames emanating from it, which is the spirit of consciousness that connects to the *Akashic field*. Here is where the resonant frequency of the teacher can access this *heavenly* process via the appropriate vibration emanating from their *Being*.

His right foot represents *Earth*, which is magnetic, that

actually holds down the pettiness of the mind under its pressure, by virtue of its upper center being in true communion with the planet. The leg that is risen depicts the electric-vacuous nature that is hidden within, as you have seen in his personification on many altars in people's homes. These principles, in their entirety, are what I will introduce you to, as you become familiar with my teachings.

We will talk about this in detail when you are more mature. Maybe," said Master Turya, smiling.

"Until then, we have these young saplings to attend to. In seven years from now, when they start blooming, I would ask you to take every bud off all of the branches before the blossoms even start opening to flower. Begin as soon as you see they are capable of being picked without damaging the delicate foliage."

"Master, why should we take the buds off in seven years?" the young boys asked.

"I will explain that to you when that time comes," the Old Sage replied, gently smiling. "These eight saplings will be tended to, as instructed, for the first eight years, and, during this period of time, the ninth you will allow to bud early. This one will be separated from the others in terms of how we tend to it."

Hearing the Grove Master's instructions, the boys were filled with youthful anticipation. Seeing their enthusiasm, he said to them, "You must tend to these *Beings* as if they were yourself, an extension of your heart."

THE IMMATURE SEED

Seven years went by and the young boys diligently followed the instructions of the Mango Grove Master. They proceeded to watch the ninth mango tree flower early, whilst they lovingly attended the old grove, as well as carefully taking the buds off the other eight young plants.

Soon the boys, now teenagers, noticed that the lone mango tree, after blossoming, was immediately tended by many species of insects, propagating the pollination process of the bright pink clusters. As time went by, they also saw little fruits pressing forward into the world, announcing their arrival, looking like bright green marbles starting to develop from the branches.

As soon as the fruits began to appear, Master Turya said to them, "Before these mangos are fully ready, I want you to pick one of them, three or four weeks before they're ripe, and have a look at the size of the seed inside."

The boys did as they were instructed, and after they cut open the mango they had picked, they exclaimed, "Oh, the seed is so big and there's hardly any flesh."

He gently looked at them and said, "The large seed represents the abundance of youth and the reduced flesh symbolizes the lack of wisdom."

"Master, what do you mean?" one of the pupils asked.

"You must wait and be patient. The ninth tree will answer this question for you in the future. For now," the Old Sage instructed, "take all the mangos off its branches, put them into our large mortar and pestle, and crush all the kernels. The protective layers of the immature seeds are like the armor of the ignorant and must be ground into small pieces to make them more manageable to compost.

When those are broken down and have become soil, thoroughly mix it with cow dung and use that blend to fertilize all the older mango grove trees. Nothing is ever wasted," he continued. "You must remember that everything is useful. See this as a metaphor that you can apply to your life."

Hearing these wise words, one of the boys looked up and reverently asked, "What do you mean, Master? What do you mean by this?"

He looked at the teenager and said, "Everything you do and feel has an effect and is put somewhere. The question is where is it put and why, and what is necessary to let go of, and what does what you let go of become, because of this?"

"Composting of the immature husks is a metaphor for transformation of misunderstanding and signifies the symbiotic relationship between ignorance and wisdom.

Or see it this way, my young, curious disciples: Suffering becomes a form of abundant communication which is composted at the feet of the old trees in the established mango grove. And this gives them the capacity to burst forward with sweet fruit, which in actuality represents wisdom. Ignorance is sour. Wisdom is sweet," he concluded.

"You must realize, these old *Beings* are not too dissimilar from still sages, sitting quietly in their meditation of life. Their *Inaction* becomes the sweetness of their fruit, which can be seen as wheels within wheels.

When they intersect and intimately collide, like a drop of water being reunited with its source, the empty hub is informed via this pressure, and sends sensory data to the external perimeter as they softly commune, to become the words arising from the emptiness of their *Being*.

This is the eternal expression of the central axis, connected to the substance of the echoes of momentum, which allows its internal force to spin within its complex interaction with the collaborating components of the wheels.

My young friends, understand that you have to see this dimensionally as they are holographic, thus harmoniously passing through each other, without any form of resistance.

Know at this point, the Hub is the expression of *Emptiness*, of *No Place*. It is void of form yet animates from the center its wheels of *Inaction*."

"Oh, Master, you don't say anything for years, and then you say that?" one of the disciples exclaimed.

The Old Sage continued, "See it this way: Within your mind, transform this vacuous image into wood, just like the solid, three-dimensional wheels of a cart being pulled by a donkey. They can be affected by a disharmonious beast that drags it in any direction, without purpose.

This animal plays the part of an undisciplined mind that leads the cart of experience to places where it should not be, thus causing the dilemma of misunderstanding within the lives of the uninformed human beings that become afflicted by the actions of the ignorant. The cart signifies your life path or your timeline on your short journey upon this planet."

At this point the disciples jumped up and down, "Master what you are transmitting is beautiful, but how can we possibly understand what you just said?"

"The holographic wheels represent prayer, the harmonious realizations of what needs to occur before it happens," he continued. "The world whispers its mantra toward us, and we have to be sensitive enough to hear that chant.

This is why the wheels move through each other so subtly, to lift our capacity as sentient *Beings* to eventually find the source of the spokes. We must become more and more quiet within so as to realize that the hub of the wheel animates itself in a state of unique perfection that echoes through the three-dimensional world; and this soundwave bounces through our reality as our *Inactions* begin to do what truly needs to be done.

A prayer cannot be prayed, nor can it be thought. It cannot be spoken, unless it rises through the heart, and when one does have the capacity to speak on its behalf, it is only half of the equation.

Each intersecting point of momentum within the vibration that is occurring holds fifty percent of what is necessary to bring *Inaction* into the world of dynamic movement. This is one of the secrets of prayer. We will talk about this more in the future, but remember, prayer cannot be prayed."

One of the disciples curiously intervened and asked, "Why is it only half of the information, Master? What do you mean by this?"

The Old Sage looked at the boy and explained, "The information that can be described as sensory data is always held in abeyance by the environment. The question is: Can you discover what you can't feel, can you locate what you can't see, can you touch what cannot be felt?

This is one of the essential elements that surround the concept of prayer, which in this case, is to be understood as transmission.

Look at it this way. When the mango tree flowers, is that not its mantra to attract insects for the pollination process to occur? What a flower can teach you is that you must not have motive. The pre-emptive force of your expectation must not be there. Know this: It took eons for the flower bud to manifest as the expression of its unwavering devotion to its environment.

In other words, an immature intellect will never comprehend what is necessary to be understood. The donkey is smart, but what type of intelligence are we dealing with? That is the issue. We all know they are very stubborn, just like the mind when it's convinced it's right, isn't it so?" said Master Turya, laughing.

"This is a destructive form of wheels within wheels that we must avoid," he continued. "These spokes made of timber may seem reasonable, but do they make any sense? Look at the world around you when you enter the village. See if you can identify this reasonableness that surrounds you, without saying a word to anyone and without judging what you witness.

In the first set, the wheels are holographic; in the second, they are solid wood. When these highly solidified spokes collide, from a reasonable perspective, great destruction and turmoil follow as a consequence of calling this destiny towards ourselves as a community. This has implications that are not realized until it is too late, for these spokes are not supple enough to see that change can occur without conflict.

The wooden wheels of the cart that is dragged by the donkey represent collisions between people upon the intersection of life. Realize, the ass," the Master said, laughing, "which is your internal dialogue that never ceases its repertoire, is a false voice, a Trojan horse. Nevertheless, my young friends, I will further explain this principle to you in the future.

Wisdom arises from the holographic hub and is always expressed from the heart. Also, the rivers of our consciousness do not speak. They flow through the body like harmonious tributaries that find the truest place to settle in comparison to the internal environment. We must be like water, but as you know, it never argues with a rock; it simply flows around it while observing the resistant phenomena.

The mysteriousness of wisdom will re-emerge within your memory to inform you where you are in comparison to where you were, which is right now. Do not worry that you cannot understand me at this moment. As you grow into vibrant young men, my present words at this point in time will transform into your realizations within your future.

So, this is your first journey into the concept of *Not Doing* versus *Doing*, but at the moment this will be tentative for you, as you still have much to learn at the level of your body, not your mind."

The next two years quickly passed by and the Master of the Mango Grove at this crucial point said to the teenagers, "Now that you are eighteen, it's time to let the immature mango tree bud again."

Sure enough, the pink clusters soon bloomed into radiant flowers, calling to all insects to come pollinate them. Seeing this, the Grove Master said, "This season, I want you to let the mangos grow to full size and allow them to completely ripen. Then, when this occurs, I would like you to pick one and bring it to me."

While this was happening, the other eight trees in the mango grove were still not permitted to bear fruit. The boys noticed the roots of these plants were becoming substantial, their branches strong. They were just very beautiful *Beings* patiently waiting for the time when they could truly flourish.

A couple of months later, the boys brought one ripe fruit from the ninth tree to the Grove Master, and he said to them, "I would like you to cut it open now and taste it."

The boys opened-up the ripe mango and they noticed the seed was still a little bit too big and the flesh wasn't that abundant. "Master, this looks beautiful, and it smells wonderful."

"Well, now I want you to try it," he said. They tasted the mango for the first time, and their faces grimaced, and they exclaimed in disappointment, "Oh Master, this mango is terribly sour!"

Having presented the boys with the experience of the sour mango, Master Turya said, "I want you to continue to take all the buds off this tree for the next few years and do the same with the other eight so that they don't bear fruit."

PATIENTLY WAITING

Another two years passed by peacefully. The boys were becoming strong young men, and it was now approaching the end of the prescribed timespan of eleven years. The Grove Master gathered them together under the Bodhi tree and announced, "It is finally time to allow the buds to become flowers, and therefore all the nine mango trees will be capable of bearing fruit."

The young men were watching and waiting and still wondering to themselves impatiently why the fruit from the separated plant was sour.

When the young mango grove was full of fruit, ready to

be harvested, the Old Sage directed them, "Now I want you to pick some mangos from these eight trees and bring them to me."

Master Turya was wise. He knew the men were very similar to these eight plants; they were strong and flexible and internally rich, yet they did not know what this abundance was within them. Their roots were deep, but they did not realize the vastness of their substance yet. They had been observing and waiting, just like the eight trees.

The disciples knew that the mangos from the one that matured too early were sour, the seeds a bit too big, and the flesh a little too lean.

They opened up the fruit from the harvest where the trees hadn't been allowed to blossom into full flourishing abundance until now. When they cut it open, they noticed that the seed wasn't that big and the flesh was full.

The Grove Master said to them, "Please, smell this before you taste it."

They smelled the vibrant mango, and you could plainly

see the look of pleasure and wonder on their faces. The young men became truly joyful inside, and exclaimed, "Oh, Master, these smell delicious!" Their mouths were watering and they said, "We would like to taste this, Master. It smells wonderful!"

The Old Sage took the mango from the men, cut it into equal portions, and gave it back to them to taste. The juice from the fruit was dripping through their fingers. They savored the sensation and were filled with delight as the mango saturated them with its vibration. "Master, this fruit is exquisite!" one of the young men exclaimed.

Smiling knowingly, the sage said, "This fruit is now becoming an acoustic phenomenon which began resonantly voicing itself through your heart so you may speak. Do you have a question for me?"

The young man said, surprised, "Yes, Master! Can you please explain further about the holographic spokes?"

"Now, you must realize—before I answer your question—that food is a form of power and it will express itself through your voice and internal realizations, which become its echo resounding through your body," the Master of the Mango Grove replied.

"Prayer, in actuality, is transmission, and even though you believe that you are asking the question, it is the mango tree's voice arising from within. Realize, even though they do not have ears, they have heard what I have said to you in the past about wheels within wheels. They know the answer to your question, but they wish you to hear it through the resonant frequency of my voice. This is how trees communicate. You are now beginning to understand the first steps of this evolutionary process.

The taste of this sweet fruit that has entered you is the prayer of the tree which is manifesting as your question for me. This is how the mango tree becomes the man. Osmosis of this kind is one of the most unique forms of empathic communion that we can ever encounter."

Having finished savoring the fruit, the Mango Grove Master instructed them, "Now go and collect some from the tree that we permitted to mature early."

The disciples did as they were requested, and when Master Turya opened these fruits, they noticed that the seed was a little bit smaller than before, and the flesh was more abundant than previously because it was a little bit older. However, when the young men smelled it, they didn't feel the same excitement as they had with the mangos from the other eight trees. "Master, why is this different?" the men asked.

Smiling, he promptly cut it into pieces, passing it back to them. They each took a bite. One of the young men, sticking his tongue out with disdain, said, "Master, this will make our teeth fall out! This fruit is sour. Even though they are totally yellow and look like they have substance, they don't! They still taste like green mangos!"

As the Grove Master voiced the philosophy behind what he had done, the men realized what he had delivered to them in terms of their experience of waiting and observing the immature fruit coming forward too early, and how the other trees blossomed within abundance because they were withheld from their ability to come forth into the world too soon.

Now that they were coming into their manhood, the disciples, full of confidence and enthusiasm, wanted to know, "Master, why do we need to wait? We can see why the fruit from those eight trees became sweet, because we took the flowers from their branches, but what are you teaching us with these two elements that give us such different results?"

The sage was wise and experienced and did not falter as the men tried to extract answers from him. "Well," he said, "I still want you to wait for five more years as you tend with devotion the mango grove and the single tree that you allowed to flower too early."

The young men, full of spunk, knowing that they couldn't get the Old Sage to answer their questions said, "Yes Master, we'll do as you say." Nonetheless, they were so pent up with curiosity and would often ask, "Why, Master, why can't we know?"

ABUNDANCE

Time continued to roll by, and after five years had passed, the Grove Master brought the young men together for a meeting under the Bodhi tree.

"The mango grove has provided so much bliss and happiness to the people of this village, and so much abundance has been shared with the poor, thanks to the plentiful harvests. But as you know, the population of our village has expanded, and even if the grove does supply beautiful fruit, it's no longer enough to feed our growing community." The young men, who had been patiently waiting for this moment and could no longer contain their curiosity, barely paid attention to what the Old Sage had said about the village.

"Well, Master, it's been five years. You're meant to tell us why we had to wait! And why did we let the single mango tree ripen before the others? Please explain to us Master. Why?!"

Touching the shoulder of one of his disciples, Master Turya bent over, holding his tummy, laughing, and answered, "You men are so focused on finding out what I haven't told you yet, that what I have just explained seems to have gone over your head. It is more important now to teach you how to increase the yield of the mango grove, instead of answering this question."

"Well," said the Grove Master, softly giggling as he wiped tears away from his eyes, "there is still one more lesson that I must share with you before revealing the secret of the sour mango tree. We need more fruit because there are now more people in the village, and therefore I must demonstrate to you how to influence the grove to produce a greater yield, at least twenty-five to thirty percent more than in the previous seasons."

He fetched a big machete and turned to them with a crazy look in his eye as he comically shook it over his head, proclaiming, "Now, I will show you how we will ask these trees to give us more!" The apprentices watched their Master's unexpected antics, not knowing what was going on.

"Come with me," he said, walking purposefully towards the old grove.

They followed him, and upon arriving he handed a machete to each of them saying, "I want you to observe what I am going to do next. This is how this mango tree will be given the message that it must produce more fruit because there is not enough to feed the people in our village."

The Old Sage took his machete and showed his disciples that it wasn't absolutely sharp, and it wasn't blunt either. "This is very important," he said, "so that they will not be overly impacted by what we are going to do next."

The Grove Master then proceeded to the orchard with the young men following him. He went up to the most abundant tree in the grove and chopped it several times from its base up to the height of his mid-chest. Chop, chop, chop, once at the front of the tree, and then, walking halfway around it, chop, chop, chop, at the back of it with the machete.

Shocked, one of the apprentices asked, "Why, Master, are you trying to kill it?"

The Old Sage replied, "No, I'm not killing it. I'm asking this tree to yield more fruit, under the threat of duress.

The machete represents the harshness of the trials and tribulations of life. When we are challenged like this, we become more abundant and versatile in terms of our ability to survive adversity. Our ingenuity is like the tree becoming more productive, bearing fruit that will give rise to another sapling.

This, in essence, is our creative ability to sustain ourselves in situations that seem overwhelming. Obstacles make us stronger and more resourceful, in terms of intelligently applying ourselves to the wooden spokes of our timeline."

"The same happens to the mango tree," Master Turya continued. "Because it does not want to be defeated by the machete, it produces more fruit. Now go do this to all the other trees in the old grove except for the nine you have tended for so many years. They are not mature enough to handle this yet," he added.

"As you're aware, youngsters of our community are not faced with this type of adversity either. And we know, by virtue of our experience, that they cannot be burdened with this sort of stress. Similarly, the young mango tree trunks are not that large, and if a machete were to impact them, it would go too deep and would do irreversible harm to their core.

In like manner, we know the innocence of the young can be damaged by the pressure of too much responsibility, to such a degree that their happiness would bleed into sorrow, thus daunting their ability to see the world with the internal buffer of their youthful exuberance which will transform into the positivity of their capacity to deal with life when they are older."

ABUNDANCE

The Mango Grove Master stopped in the middle of this explanation and stated, "There is an ancient technique pertaining to weapons that was well known, deep in the history of the old world. Remind me to transmit this secret to you in the future."

"Oh, not another thing that we have to wait for!" the disciples exclaimed, grinning at one another joyfully as they went away and diligently began giving cuts to all the trees in the old grove.

The next growing season, the young devotees noticed that every single tree was yielding twenty-five to thirty percent more fruit because of what they had done the previous year.

Once the harvest was done and all the ripe fruit was picked and stored in bamboo baskets, the apprentices gathered under the shade of the Bodhi tree, and asked the Old Sage, "Master, wouldn't it have been prudent to have allowed the weight of the mangos to bring substance to the strength of the branches of all those eight trees during these years?"

"What you say sounds reasonable," he replied. "However, these trees have adapted very quickly to the heaviness of the mangos they produced when we gave them permission to bear fruit after so much time. They are just like me, my devoted disciples.

So many years I have waited before I was asked to take responsibility for your consciousness. This was not a burden for me. It was a joy, thus revealing the capacity of my *Inaction* to bear sweet fruit within my ability to communicate what I have withheld, because I had never been asked."

Looking at his disciples, who were really excited to hear more, Master Turya asked them, "What was your experience with the ninth mango tree and how it bore fruit long before the others were harvested?"

"Well, Master, the one that fruited first seems to be feeble and weak, even though its branches were allowed to hold weight before the harvest of the other eight. The seeds were bigger and the flesh was not as abundant, so its branches weren't bearing as much weight as the trees in the old grove were.

We can see now that the single tree became used to not carrying the full impact of what it was meant to, had it also waited for those many years to pass by."

Another of the young men asked, "Master, why is this such a strong contradiction? Why is this tree weaker even though it bore fruit earlier? Why doesn't it seem as lustrous? Why aren't the leaves as attractive?"

"The weakness of the ninth tree lies in its inability to bear sweet fruit," the Old Sage responded cryptically. "This is the only clue I'll offer you now."

The young men looked at each other with large smiles on their faces, knowing that the Grove Master would not be giving in, no matter how much they implored him to, so they would have to wait.

I AM A MOUNTAIN, I AM

Many seasons passed, and the men, who were now in their mid-twenties, came to the Old Sage and said, "Master, we have so much fruit and abundance, so much sweetness and happiness in our village, and we can see that what you have done is very wise and purposeful.

You've cared for many by instructing us on how to gather the best of our harvest and teaching us to patiently wait for the outcome of what needs to occur, over so many years. But Master, how can we share what you have taught us, when we have no words yet to explain?"

Master Turya, now well into his old age, said, "You've

waited for so long, and you're becoming quite substantial strong men. You walk with firmness. Your roots are deep, and your hearts reach towards the sky. You have fortitude and patience. Your eyes are wise to watch very carefully for the abundance around you, but still, you have no words to speak of what you know."

"My loving friends," he continued, "you need to do one other thing, without me telling you why."

They looked upon their Master with reverence and quieted their minds to listen.

"I want you to repeat something to yourself and not to attempt to fathom the meaning of what I am imparting but to live the feeling of this teaching, without any explanation. What I will give you is a mantra."

The men waited excitedly to hear the precious words that their Master was about to share with them.

"You will not look for the outcome of this," he advised. "You will live the mantra within your *Being* and understand, *I am a Mountain, I AM*."

As he spoke, the Grove Master was carefully observing his young disciples. They were becoming, indeed, very strong and competent human beings. Their actions in the village were good and kind, only giving the best of themselves, never seeking recognition or expecting reward for what they had done.

"Master," they asked, "will you tell us why you gave us this mantra?"

The Old Sage, with a mischievous smile which they recognized well, said to them, "You'll have to wait for two more seasons to find out why I have given you this."

Still, they had further questions, "Master, how should we really practice this mantra?"

Again, the Old Sage said to them, "*I am a Mountain, I AM*. You must never imagine saying to yourself, *I am the Mountain, I AM*. *I am a Mountain, I AM*, is what you're meant to say."

Not fully understanding what their Master had just conveyed to them, the disciples insisted, "But why, Master, should we say, *I am a Mountain, I AM*, and not, *I am the Mountain, I AM?*"

Master Turya looked at them with his steady gaze and replied, "*I am the Mountain*, is the young sapling that was allowed to flower too early, and *I am a Mountain, I AM* is the representation of the mango trees that we brought to true fruition."

With their eyes widening in realization, the men said to their Master, "We understand about the mango tree that delivers sour fruit. Are we to consider that it believes it is *the Mountain*? And that the trees that yield the sweet fruit, say to themselves *I am a Mountain, I AM?*"

The Master of the Mango Grove smiled lovingly and said, "I will release one more precious secret to you: The sour mango tree operates through motive. The sweet mango trees have no motive. They have already arrived."

A further two seasons passed. The powerful young men were now honored in the village and everyone loved them dearly.

They came to their teacher, who by now was very elderly, and spoke reverently to him, "Master, can you please reiterate why you have instructed us about the mango trees in such detail, over so many years? Your teachings have made us feel very strong and happy. How and why has this happened?

And the mantra, you still haven't fully revealed to us why we had to say it. And why is *a Mountain* different from *the Mountain*? Why is *the Mountain* sour, and *a Mountain* sweet? Why is *the Mountain* full of preconception or with motive? Why does *a Mountain* symbolize not having motive? And why does the mantra reflect such a different feeling to the single mango tree in comparison to the others that are full of abundance? Can you explain that to us?"

The Master smiled that smile they had become so used to. "Yes, I can explain all of these things to you, but we are going to have to wait for another two seasons."

The spirited disciples looked at him and laughed, saying, "Master, you're such a devil! We have grown-up, and now we have wives and children, and everyone in the village loves us so much.

We say that we have learned all of the ways of living within abundance from the man who owns the mango grove, the Master of acting and not speaking. We've come to terms with the fact that we have to wait, but can you, please, give us a hint of what we're going to learn, after two more seasons of waiting?"

With a twinkle in his eyes, the Old Sage looked upon them lovingly. "You're going to learn about *Being, Knowing, and Not Doing* what you think you know," he said, then added, "What you will discover will absolutely relate to why the flowers were diligently taken from the eight trees for so many years. We have to explore these concepts that you lovingly put into action before we go back to the original lessons that I imparted many seasons ago."

Two years later, full of anticipation, the men came to their Master's side while he was sitting under the Bodhi tree.

"Master Turya, what are the principles of *Being, Knowing, and Not Doing*?" they asked collectively.

Inviting them to gather around, he said, "It's time I tell you why I instructed you to allow the mango tree to flower too early and why you've been carrying out these teachings faithfully, almost half your life now.

But to explain everything, first, we have to retrace our tracks through the history of the mango grove and of the nine trees that you planted so many years ago. Within this are the reasons why it is so important to pluck the flowers and not allow them to become fruit too early. This puts the eight saplings in a state of *Not Doing*, and this is the first secret that the young mango grove reveals to us."

The disciples sat there riveted to the words of their teacher as he continued.

"During your life, I have asked you not to comment, not to judge, and not to be in scorn of anybody else's *Being*, but to see them within the light of your own abundance. And as they reveal themselves to you, I have asked you not to have any thoughts within yourself nor feelings that arise from your contact with them and not to ever give advice in any way whatsoever, even if you have deep realizations about their circumstances.

I instructed you to take inside what you notice and not to ever speak of it. In other words, you must pluck the flowers of your own momentary insights and wait patiently until your wisdom arrives appropriately as the years go by.

As I have asked you to do all these things, you've noticed that you've become like the sturdy trees from which you removed the budding flowers. Those *Beings* waited for a very long time to have the possibility of yielding the most abundant, sweet fruits that would nourish our village, and they did so without asking for anything in return."

As they absorbed these teachings, the men began wiping tears of gratitude from their faces.

"Each tree within the mango grove is *Being* ultimately in a state of *Knowing* what surrounds it, and as it cannot move, nor avoid anybody coming into its presence, it cannot judge. If it condones its own bias at that particular point, its roots will have no substance nor the ability to profoundly connect with the wisdom of transformation via this *Doing*, which never would be *Done* by an ancient tree," the Old Sage added.

In response to hearing these words, the men looked at each other and said, "Master, this is so amazing! We've never really realized until this point what you have done. But can you tell us, as we don't quite understand, what has the sour mango tree got to do with all of this?"

The Master of the Mango Grove, very patient and wise, looked at them and replied, "Remember, the flower buds represent the manifestation of the possibility of a *Doing* coming forward prematurely. This is a declaration of their *Knowing*, which is, in actuality, false wisdom. And that flower will only create sourness through its pre-emptive immaturity."

"Youth, in a lot of cases, is wasted within the young," the Master concluded.

"The eight trees in the new grove know of this because you have diligently removed the flower buds from their limbs so they can wait steadfastly to appear in their strongest form in the years to come, thus experiencing this as a *Not Doing* of their potential *Doing* being held back via this act. This represents, in our lives, a form of restraint that is in many cases, recognized too late.

I will explain these principles in more depth in the future and how opportunities lost are, in actuality, beneficial. This echoes back to the kernels of the immature fruits that are never wasted and which you crushed in our mortar and pestle into small pieces to be more easily managed in the composting process."

Master Turya smiled and continued, "The real lesson you are learning here is to order your mind in a very functional manner to see that there are pragmatic ways to proceed. This will educate your body not to become preoccupied with unnecessary thoughts, for they are a true waste of one's life energy.

We all must learn to be practical and purposeful and only deal with what is necessary and do that in a positive manner. By acting this way, your mind becomes orderly and will not miss its opportunity to be constructive."

The men were listening, absorbed in a deep silence while their Master lovingly carried on, "This is why I said to you years ago: Look within the people that live in our village but do not judge them. They are only suffering a minor affliction, and this is not noticing that they are being irrational with their rationality or being negative when they could be positive. You are very close now to understanding the explanation of the sour mango tree. I have given you half the information already."

"We are so grateful, Master, that you are sharing this truth with us." Unable to contain their excitement, the disciples insisted, "Please, tell us more!"

"The immature mango tree represents a person who is very young in their development, even if they're advanced in years. They may have read many books and believe that they know something, for knowledge can be repeated verbatim, as a false truth to reveal itself in the turmoil of life.

The young tree announces, *My flowers look beautiful and I bear fruit, and I will underhandedly relay this information to you as it fits delicately into your circumstances while I assure you of my vanity without you knowing.*

The symbolism of the sour fruit that appears after the beautiful flower declares: *Here is where a mango will reside and appear for you who see this opening bud* is to reveal its pre-emptive motive to bring forth knowledge that is not wise.

Behind the declaration of the immature plant, there is always scorn, jealousy, competitiveness, and unruliness. It will defend its perspective, its false wisdom, with all the elements that are not meant to be there. This is the reason why I asked you to pick the flowers from the eight mango trees to ensure that they don't come forth too early."

Master Turya then added, "If they bloom too soon, they profess they know something they don't, which is only their immaturity wishing to be acknowledged for the false trials and tribulations of life that they claim to have experienced, which they have not." The men were silent, listening attentively to his every word.

"The flower is a very interesting element of the mango tree," the Old Sage continued, "It reveals its fragrance, its shape, beauty and color, and these features are what draws everybody to it. This represents the vanity and pride of internal immaturity. Since the flowers of the immature tree are no different to those of a mature plant, it still draws to itself the response of the eyes and the feelings of other *Beings* to say, *The mango tree is flowering.*

Nevertheless, as it buds and begins to bear fruit, it doesn't yet have substance. As you know, however, the sour fruit is used for different purposes, like the exotic salads that our chefs ingeniously adapt into delicious dishes. This shows us the sharp eye of the wise, recognizing unripe consciousness and putting it to practical use, thus turning this imposition into a *Not Doing*.

Even though there are negatives in life, my devoted disciples, we can always shift things away from being offended into a constructive *Not Doing*, and, as this occurs, our personal timeline will arise as a seed that will bud appropriately into each *Being's* uniqueness, similarly to what you see in a field of flowers. There are many different colors that emanate from varying species that draw your feelings to the individual timelines of the people you are meant to meet on your path," the Old Sage elucidated.

"Master, what you are explaining is brutally honest within its perfection," the disciples exclaimed. "We deeply appreciate the time and effort that you have put into this aspect of our lives. Still, could you please say more about how you came upon the inspiration of *I am a Mountain, I AM*—the mantra that you gave us? And also, how did you become so patient and wise?"

The Master of the Mango Grove looked up and replied, "I'd love to tell you how I came across the concept of *the Mountain*. But first I want to describe the details of how I met my Master in Tibet when I was a child, as a pilgrimage of my devotion towards him. It was he who originally conveyed the Mountain story to me as a young boy."

MY TEACHER

As the years went by, a profound silence permeated the old grove as a consequence of the concentrated meditative influence emanating from the Master and his disciples. Seated around the Bodhi tree, having completed their morning practice, they were all patiently waiting for the Old Sage to begin the story he had promised he would tell.

His voice resonated with blissful enthusiasm as he gently looked upon his disciples. "My Master was a very subtle, kind monk. He taught me many things. Before revealing to you some of these stories, I would like to tell you why I gifted you a machete in the beginning of your apprenticeship with me.

As you recall, when you first became my pupils in the mango grove, I gave each of you a knife and asked you to wear it at all times. You may have noticed that most of the farmers in our community keep these sharp implements tucked in their belt or casually carry them in their hands, in between their duties. Though this is common practice, it's hardly ever noticed. But it does have a profound effect.

If you remember, as I know you do, my loving disciples, I asked you all to strap your machetes to your hips while undertaking all your tasks within the mango grove for all these years. There was a specific reason why I instructed you to do this.

When wearing the knife, your body feels strong and secure. The weapon represents protection and the readiness to act in your circumstance immediately when you see something that needs to be done. The machete was not to be kept in the shed; it was always by your side, within the purpose of your actions here in the grove.

When you meet another disciple and they, too, have their machete sheathed, it shows your strength and reveals a threat simultaneously, even though there is no conflict. Both elements cause your immunity to become stronger, and this is the ultimate reason why I asked you to wear these tools.

In the old world this custom was well known as an ancient form of power. But remember, when I say this, I am not talking about dominance. It is something else that arises from the act of wearing this sacred object, in comparison to the liquid consciousness of the bearer.

In times past, human beings were more aware of these subtleties via realizing that the act of *Not Doing* appears as a manifestation of their *Doings*, which, in reality, is true education.

Recognizing what can be known via the acoustic revelation, in essence, is the prayer of the body to the transdimensional *Being* that is travelling within it. And this is another form of communion, a subtlety that is deeply hidden within our empathic nature."

"Master, what you say is so beautiful!" a disciple exclaimed. "I am now beginning to comprehend more about the way you teach!"

Hearing this, Master Turya started laughing joyously. "I have taught you to allow the rivers of your mind to flow through your body, as unrestricted tributaries that may come upon your internal resistances, via the people you have witnessed during your early apprenticeship with me. Do you remember?"

"Yes, Master, we do remember," one of the men answered. "It is like water travelling around a rock and not conversing with what it has discovered, only noticing the resistance," he added.

The Old Sage smiled affectionately and continued with his explanation. "In this case, it's not the resistances within that you are becoming aware of. It is the external phenomenon or the challenges outwardly expressed by your environment that will wish to provoke you to formulate a *Knowing* which you must immediately transform into a *Not Doing* so as not to be caught by the illusion presenting itself in the guise of other people's circumstances.

This neutral stance transforms the dogma that is held within the body as a point of reference, created primarily by the mind's insistence to adhere rigidly to the bias programmed into its consciousness.

Similarly, over the years, I have asked you to do the same thing within your external actions. Concentrate with sincerity towards all *Beings* of light you may come in contact with so you may develop a level of devotion that would wish *never to do harm to another* that exists within this diversity which you are experiencing on your individual timelines with me, here in the grove. Nevertheless, let's get back to the story of my teacher."

PATHWAYS OF MY MEMORY

In a powerful and kind voice, the Old Sage began, "Now, I wish to tell you a beautiful tale from my childhood, about how I met my Master—a mysterious Tibetan monk. This is how I came upon these profound understandings that I am transmitting to you, my loving disciples. It is a story of how to reach devotion without having motive.

As a small boy, growing up in a village in Tibet, I wanted to go live in a temple and learn from the monks there. So I said to my mother and father, 'I would like to become a disciple.' Seeing the sincerity of my determination, my parents were honored and very happy that their five-year-old son wished to study with a Master.

Joyfully, they hugged me and said, 'This is wonderful, son. We will take you to the temple and ask the head monk if it's possible for you to enter and be under his tutelage.'

Several weeks later, we were at the entrance of the monastery when the head monk communicated to my parents that once I was admitted, there would be no more contact. He said to them that I had to be initiated into a certain way of being which undoes everything that I was previously accustomed to.

After informing my parents that they could retrieve me at the age of twenty-one, the monk, smiling, looked me in the eyes, and opened his hands very gently, beckoning me to come towards him. As I was slowly walking, my eyes wide open, I saw the Master softly raise his finger to his lips, indicating not to say a word. He then gestured to follow him, and at this point I realized I was being introduced to the routines within the Temple.

The first thing he showed me was to take off my shoes

and walk very quietly up to the entrance. Then, looking at me, he smiled and touched my hand softly while he, again, put his finger to his lips to instruct me to be very quiet and unobtrusive.

He opened the door very slowly and beckoned me to come in after him. Then he took my hand tenderly, put it on the handle and asked me, by gestures not by words, to very lightly close it so we didn't make a sound.

We quietly went into the meditation room. The first thing he instructed me to do was to sit down next to him. Gently gazing at its interior, I could see it didn't seem like anybody noticed we had entered, but everybody was very aware that somebody was there, even though no sound was made.

After some time in meditation, the old monk guided me through the gardens of the temple, and then proceeded to show me where all the paths were located and how they weaved in between all the buildings within the property.

My first task at morning light was to arise and sweep

these cobblestones thoroughly clean. The mysterious old Tibetan had instructed me to be gentle and quiet within my duties so as not to disturb the singular awarenesses of all the devotees emerging from their early morning meditation within their dormitories.

At this point, only the sound of my devotion would be felt within the hearts of the monks, and this is the first lesson of unification that I became aware of as a child."

The Master of the Mango Grove lovingly observed his disciples listening intently to his recounting of his childhood for them, and then added, "Speaking it to you in this present moment is different to knowing it then. I am more complete now and understand why the old Tibetan educated me in such a beautiful manner. My childhood teacher guided me in this way so I could connect the abundance of my heart to the expansiveness of his open *Beingness* towards me.

What he was revealing to my young tenderness was that the flowers and leaves upon the path depict struggle and ease inside the memories that possess us all within our past. When they are swept from our view, it is as if they never existed and this represents the letting go of what once was so that one can appear as who they really are, not what they were.

When you arrive in this elusive position, the lotus flower of *No Place* then reveals to you what is truly there: your act of devotion.

This is subsequently applied to the monks themselves. No matter what they have achieved within their meditations and discipline, the only thing that really exists for them in the morning is a clear path that is not encumbered by who they think they are in comparison to who they were.

In other words, to be somebody we must reduce ourselves to the impression of nothing or nobody. And this is how I learned to come upon the *divine*."

"My devoted disciples," Master Turya continued, "this is the way the Tibetan monk transmitted the philosophy that was behind what he was teaching so as to speed up my comprehensive reflection."

One of the disciples, hearing this beautiful story, said to him, "Now we understand more deeply, Master, why you

+ 354 7699940

~~7999~~

Hanse

STAÐGREITT

Dags.	20	KRÓNUR
	SAMTALS	

carefully instructed us to be so caring and dedicated to the process of the mango grove."

The Old Sage lovingly resumed his elucidation, "This act of devotion, which was a doing of my body, was to undo the actions of the night so that the monks could walk upon the clear path, which automatically became their clarity towards their purpose of the day.

You must remember, they themselves once used to be the children of the Temple, sweeping the same paths. Within their heart they did not even reflect upon what had been done, but they remembered what they did, which in actuality, allowed me to become their memory. This is how we became *One Being*. I became them as they recognized me, and this is how we transform separation into unification. '*We are all One Being,*' the Tibetan Master used to say, '*you just have to realize it.*'

In retrospect, I see that my purpose was to be confronted with flowers and then with the emptiness and perfection of that path, so others may walk upon the softness of my intentions. This, for me as a child, was beautiful. But let's get back to the story, my beloved disciples.

On the completion of my first daily task, I would go to the kitchen to carry on with my morning duties. The Tibetan Master would always accompany me, when he was teaching what was required of me in terms of how to respond, and he would gently show me what to do.

When the monks prepared food, as soon as waste was created it was immediately discarded into the composting bin and mixed with soil so as to fertilize the beautiful gardens of the monastery.

Once that was done, I was to bring all the bowls and place them one by one, in reverence, in front of all the elderly ascetics that lived in this temple. Meanwhile, the head chef, lovingly nicknamed 'Cookie,' was preparing my meal in the kitchen as I was finishing. He would hand me my food and we would join the others and sit down.

Nobody would eat until we all arrived. They were very generous in terms of their patience, and there was no shame, no blame and no guilt. There was nothing to be done but to wait for the moment when we could all eat.

Before this occurred, the mutual respect between everybody was absolutely tangible. Yet for the untrained eye this would not be obvious. The reverence that was so abundant filled our *Being* with gratitude, which spread between all of us instantly and gave the event of simply eating a feeling of timelessness that became overwhelmingly evident through our silent prayer of *Inaction*.

At this point, I noticed many of the monks practicing mudras, gesturing their hands over the food to imbue it with the emptiness that radiated the beauty of their hearts before this nourishment entered their bodies. Such subtleties can never be forgotten.

As soon as they finished eating and there was an empty bowl, I would immediately take it back to the kitchen to be cleaned and put away where it originally came from—never in a different location, always back in the same spot. So I was taught that once something was done, it was cleansed and stored, awaiting to be used the next day, as if it had never been moved.

While the monks proceeded with their daily rituals which included chanting, meditations, and movement, I perceived energy emanating from the bowls in the kitchen, noticing me as if their stillness was animated, as a reflection of my studious duty to the room.

This is when I realized that the character of that space reflected me and everybody that entered it. The chambers of the temple as a whole have a personality that rings like a soft bell. It is important we only add devotion to them, for anything left behind returns to the sender.

This is what I was taught by the Master: that the inner space of one's lodgings is like a person. Its eyes, its feelings contain you and, as you are surrounded by the walls and the ceiling, you are embraced by yourself. You call upon it, and it calls upon you.

This is one of the secrets that the mysteriousness of my time with these Masters revealed. Their eyes became the room; their feelings saturated the walls. Thus, they reflected back the same attitude that I was taught to emanate. Caring love and devotion calls to itself love and devotion.

As I am, so the room becomes. As the room is, so am I. This is how I learned about the first teaching of Buddha and how the world calls upon me as I call upon it.

This routine went on for years. So I became like cloth, saturated in the water that cleanses it: soaked and dried, soaked and dried, until the garment that I wore truly became me.

We were all cleaning and organizing the inner spaces and preparing things for certain activities, and within this magical coordination, everybody's duty was done perfectly.

Simultaneous realizations became the outcome of everybody's intention, which naturally fulfilled all the elements so harmoniously, through observation of what needed to be done. This was never spoken of nor debated upon.

As the time went by, my body realized how the pressure of one would affect the outcome of the others. I learned over the years that what needed to be done becomes the image within my mind of the room that I would enter. Upon my arrival, it would speak to my heart and show me how to proceed.

As I tell this story to you, my loving disciples, I am still doing the same thing. The difference is that I enter these rooms of the past inside the temple of my mind. Traveling through these memories, it calls upon me to speak of it in transmission of these events, given to you with caring devotion in response to your attention upon me.

As this occurs, you enter the inner spaces of your homes within the village, and as my past calls upon my voice to speak to you, your present reality reveals your rooms to you and shows you what is there.

My dear friends, each of you has a different house, a different feeling, and a different family. You are now learning to travel to your present moments via my memory. As you see me, you discover yourselves within the diverse elements that call upon your reflection to enact your challenges upon what reveals itself to you.

This is the teaching of Buddha—*As others are, so am I*. It

is a form of communion, an empathic realization that asks you to speak to the world through wordlessness. And this is the second revelation of Buddha's teachings that was transmitted to me by my Master.

His timeline, which in actuality is his lifetime, entered the container of my cargo ship and has taught me the most precious secret there is, that I am now transmitting to you. Whatever poured into my cup now transfers into yours. What flows from you into others is like my Master's cargo ship travelling within the waters from one container to another. It will move through you in comparison to your individual timelines."

Master Turya looked upon his loving devotees and further elaborated, "The power of our communion, no matter how subtle, will be understood and applied, and that outcome reveals everybody's destiny throughout their lifetime.

My dear friends, even if one does no harm and one's gestures are full of love and devotion, dropping this pebble into somebody else's pond will have different effects in comparison to the depths and breadths of another's shoreline, which is comparable to the reflective internal contours of their timeline. This represents the ripples of this drop of love into their waters. In other words, everybody's destiny individually differs. And this is the principle of the Tiger, which I have yet to explain.

This is the reason why you may have difficulties with the concept of *Harm no one, nor have them harmed*. Because, no matter what you do in loving devotion to your circumstances, the ultimate outcome cannot be foreseen. And if misfortune occurs, it is the calling of one's destiny intertwined with the love that has been shared."

The disciples were enthralled by his magical story and one of them said, "Master, can you please repeat Buddha's saying again?"

The Old Sage said, "*As I am, so are others; as others are, so am I. Having thus identified self and others, harm no one, nor have them harmed.*"

"As I matured, I realized that I had been in the temple

for nearly twenty-five years, and everything that was required of me there had only increased my feelings of devotion. What came upon me was the profound significance of what it meant to place a cup of tea in front of somebody to quench their thirst.

The feelings that I received from the old monks were their gratitude and love towards me for allowing them to be seated within their purpose, and that carried me into the delicate emanations of who they were. I was in the sincere process of being there for them, and they were in the devotional practice of being there for me, even though the object of their concentration was within.

When they travelled into the complexity of themselves, that would create a catalyst. The depth of myself would open up upon the response of whatever I felt inside of my body as I came into the room when they were meditating, or when I was being of service to them. Realize, my dear disciples, this is sincerity itself. It was the most precious time of my life, and I cherished every moment.

Still, it was time for me to go back to the village. I went

to the head monk and said to him, 'Master, I don't know exactly what I've learned, but I've greatly enjoyed my time here. I wish to re-enter the world and discover what the rest of my life has in store for me.'

The Tibetan Master knew precisely what I was going through, and he replied, 'You are free to go back to your village, and you're welcome to come back here whenever you consider it's time. If you don't return, it doesn't really matter. As long as your path is clear and open, you will be fine.'

Kindness emanated from him as he continued, 'Conceive of this before you leave. It's difficult to understand how far you've progressed, as you have been accompanied by a group of masterful people from your childhood until now. You did what you had to do, and everybody supported every element of what had to be done, so then you fell into the security of a very solid routine of *Not Doing* what usually occurs in the world that will soon surround you.

I can see your hallways of light are open, but at the moment you haven't noticed them yet. I will give you one clue. I will not tell you where they appear and how many of them are to be found, but they will reveal themselves to you like soft moonlight caressing your internal eye from within.

You will become more aware of them only upon being challenged with subtle disharmony. And this is the mountain that you will be faced with once you leave this loving refuge.'

The Grove Master's eyes shone with gratitude and affection as he recalled his teacher's words. "Let us rest now," he said. "When we meet again tomorrow, I will tell you more."

THE SHEPHERD

"My beloved disciples, the time has come to convey to you what my Master, the old Tibetan, revealed to me before I left the monastery. He said, 'What I am to share with you now, Turya, will have such a profound effect upon your awareness that it will reach into your visual matrix, which is your present world at this moment, in reflection of this transmission.

This is circular but not repetitive, as you will see. It is one of the deep, essential elements that avails itself within the empathic union between consensual *Beings*, in terms of their personal review.'

In other words, my Master's discourse, which is now my

memory, reaches into the reflection of your world to reveal to you the circumstances that deliver its visually contemplative complexities through you."

Listening to the Old Sage, the disciples felt blessed to receive more of his wisdom that was opening up so many possibilities for them to really see what needs to be applied. They patiently waited for him to continue.

"You have within your neutrality a pendulum that will indicate how to proceed, in terms of the effect of my discourse in comparison to the story of the Mountain, which I will soon describe in detail. The pendulum rocks back and forth, as well as spinning in circles inside of you, and will draw upon your memories and your internal wisdom of discernment.

You have to understand, my dear disciples, this antenna you have inside extends from your crown, travels down the very center of your physical form, and reaches the perineum at its mid-point.

Once this central line is established, then the four

directions become tangibly available, as the front and back, left and right sides begin to harmonize. To awaken this part of oneself is a complex process, but once the body realizes this axis, the lower gourd then notices its equators.

As this happens, the internal lights begin to manifest their own vibrant eddies in response to any form of movement in terms of these hallways becoming self-aware within the physical container. Eventually, the body of the initiate realizes how to follow this subtle process.

This is why I asked you in your childhood to stand still, in profound quietude, looking for the center of your lower gourd, which is regulatory within its capacity to activate whatever needs to be revealed at the moment it arises.

Be careful to understand that this description is rudimentary. I have not even explained all that exists within your upper gourd, which harmonizes itself with your balance center."

The disciples looked at their Master in amazement. What he was transmitting was so extraordinary they could hardly contain their excitement.

"Also," the Old Sage went on, "the central cylinder of light, which follows the alignment of the pendulum, is one of your major hallways which your rivers can flow through with ease.

The central channel rises from the perineal base within clockwise and anticlockwise spirals to the crown chakra, which is the zenith of the toroidal field.

Lifeforce flows back down from this upper center, mirroring the shape of your energy bubble, into the *Earth* to reunite with it. It then travels from the base of your feet into the complex mechanisms of your other hallways.

This is a highly spiritual process that you will realize as you mature into my wisdom. My description is pre-emptive to allow you to understand, from a holographic perspective, the extremely complex mechanisms of light that can be seen by the outer eyes in correspondence with the third eye, once it has opened.

If you are fortunate enough, as I have been, you will

begin to notice these hallways that appear like ribbons, pipes and pillars. They are the first stage of animation that upholds the existence of our physical representation.

This is how we arrive upon our spirit.

As a human being, it is important to understand that the process of our evolution is contingent upon a specific alignment of our internal lights. This can only be achieved by positioning our physical structure in such a way as to accommodate our original holographic functionality.

In one methodology this has been identified as *soul retrieval*, but this terminology is imprecise. It is a minor readjustment of our luminosity that we are achieving."

One of the disciples gently interrupted to ask a question. "Dear Master, what you are saying is so wonderful, but I still don't fully understand what you mean. Could you maybe explain more about these lights?"

The Old Sage lovingly agreed. "See it this way. You hold an aerial in the air above your head, trying to locate a radio frequency, adjusting your arm to make contact, searching for what you can't hear. Once this connection has been established, the station manifests, and you can listen to someone speaking within this bandwidth. Until this connection is made, you wouldn't even realize it was there.

Our body is exactly the same—you must delicately adjust it to find the signal that you didn't realize existed until sincere contact has been made. Firstly, your body will echo the *divine*. Soon after, your voice will arise within its delicate sweetness.

Hearing my words is deciphering the light of the Eternal in absolute opposition to what the mind does that has taken prisoner of the upper center. That is why I called it a Trojan horse. It organizes everything in the wrong order," the Master said, laughing.

"The internal dialogue is the sour fruit. It pretends to be sweet within its unripe declaration. This is true *Maya*, the illusion, or the false prophet. Unfortunately, at the moment, for many people on our planet, it is still there to disrupt this holy process of communing with the *divine*.

This internal diplomatic corruption takes command of our seeing center that is meant to be seated in silence, consequently turning off the third eye, and thus confusing the heart's process through coercive motives that are opposed to its original sovereignty.

The heart in actuality is the original progenitor of our intelligence. It will access the lights within, through a direct connection with the *divine* that can only echo our *beautiful, sweet, loving self.*

Our luminosity is a manifestation of the Holy Spirit. This also harkens back to the parable of forgotten innocence of Yeshua, who, as you know, once traveled through these lands. The shepherd, which is the physical body, searches for one's lost innocence, which is our light.

It is thus returned to the flock, which represents all the complex elements of consciousness. And in this story that Yeshua expresses, he states, *I care for what is lost, for without this divine communion, I am incomplete.*

This singular lamb parable has been interpreted from a

religious perspective that is extremely biased and has switched the narrative away from what it is really meant to convey.

The Shepherd is not looking for lost people. He is actually searching for his own lights, which symbolize his inner quest for himself. So then, my dear disciples, we are the Shepherd and the Lamb simultaneously. Internally, this represents recovered pages from the book of our own heart's wisdom.

In other words, retrieve that portion that has been forgotten from our scripture so we can recognize what has been lost: our inner luminescence, the lamb of our purity, our original consciousness. When this separated frequency becomes reunited with our physicality, our internal hallways then become illuminated.

This is where we discover what we can't see, can't feel, and can't touch. And when this occurs, it allows us to see it, to feel it, and embrace it, as it touches upon us.

So, my beloved devotees, as I expand on this *Inaction*, I

gently touch upon your eyes, ears, and feeling process so that you may awaken within your own path via mine.

This, in actuality, is the most difficult mountain to climb. If responded to correctly by one's inner reflectiveness, the *Being* receiving that information will be revealed to themselves via this process. The consequence of this is unwavering devotion.

In other words, a simultaneous release and realization occurs, and this is known as a form of prayer. It is an internal revelation of the truth or a true insight that reveals itself within the context of your *Inactions*."

One of the disciples, hearing about the parable of the lost lamb, asked the Old Sage, "Master, you have spoken about Yeshua many times before. Have you ever had contact with him?"

"Yes, I have," Master Turya replied, smiling. "But not in the way you would ever imagine. I will talk about this in the future. It is a subject that I have not mentioned yet, related to timeline convergence. But now, let's observe the manifestation of the story of my Mountain.

My dear disciples, before we travel further on our journey toward these peaks, I would like to prepare you, for it will reveal items that are not always what they seem. This is the beginning of our voyage into the depths of meaning, through the complex imagery that will arise within each one of you as you come into contact with the reflexive mechanisms of your own awareness.

THE MOUNTAIN

"Imagine you are at a great distance from a beautiful mountain," Master Turya began. "You are looking at it and have the feeling inside yourself of how majestic it is. You can really appreciate it from the perspective that you can see the clouds and the contours of its shape, but you can't really isolate anything.

If you're observing something from this vantage point, you would say to yourself, 'Well, I'm watching from afar. This is my capacity to proudly announce that I had contact,' where in actuality this has really not occurred."

Looking at his disciples, the Grove Master said, "Isn't

this the sour fruit? The person participating in this implies that they have climbed when they have not. This is artistry manifesting as a painted image, which we all know hasn't really happened.

When we look within the framework of this painting, we're all reminded that we have become involved visually from a standpoint of distance. Opinions are very different to experience," the Old Sage added.

"Look at it this way," he resumed. "If one were to paint Buddha and hang his portrait upon a wall, is that person a Buddhist? Even though it will draw them towards Buddhism, does this give them the capacity to read the subtleties of his journey?

That's obvious, isn't it? You appreciate the image, but have you really understood?

Does peace truly come upon you if the words from within cannot reflect the journey that you have not yet taken? At this point you must realize you possess the painting; and then does not the painting possess you?

This is the false internal recognition of one's ego. What I mean by this, my dear disciples, is that when one places a mask upon their face as an appearance, it inevitably cannot depict the image of their true heart's voice."

One of the disciples looked at him in astonishment, "What do you mean, Master? Can you please explain?"

The Old Sage, in a kind voice, resumed, "This is the tiger paw. It is similar to a big, soft, comfortable pillow that you lay your body on. In other words, it has not yet challenged anything within you. The mountain, at this point, is only a painting.

The claw of the tiger that manifests from the paw starts with a long journey towards the foot of the mountain. This is when your body begins to realize it is under duress. Simultaneously, the sun, which used to caress you, beams down insistently without mercy. The food, which you have consumed before your trip, is now challenged to come to the surface and provide your limbs with the energy necessary to complete this phase of your voyage.

Once your food energy has been depleted, then the true challenge of your power is put to its first test. It has not only worn your shoes down and weakened your knees, nightfall will soon call upon you to build your makeshift shelter to protect you from the elements. And you must have this done in a timely fashion to allow you to gather wood and light a fire while simultaneously searching for water and something to nourish your empty stomach that is already screaming for sustenance.

Remember, when you enter this challenge you cannot bring your previous *Doings* to bear relevance to the crisis that has not yet beset you. This is your *Knowings and Doings* revealing that your bare bones need to be strengthened in comparison to what is yet to come.

You brush against poison ivy and twist your ankle, since you are moving with such haste to prepare the groundwork for your fire and shelter. At this stage, your body is so involved in completing the task at hand, it has not realized it has been injured twice. My young disciples, the body has a unique shield when it is placed under duress; it turns off certain feelings in comparison to your impending trials and tribulations.

This is the pre-emptive force of nature, allowing only one moment's pause. The mountain is warning you to be diligent and calm, as it knows within the depths of its center that rushing when you should wait and pausing when you should rush is extremely dangerous."

Hearing this, one of the disciples said, "Master, I would weep if this happened to me."

"Does not the mountain itself weep? It does so by recognizing a grouping of foreboding clouds," the Old Sage replied compassionately. "This is a warning to stop and listen. Everything that is gathered within you is pent up inside this menacing image, building to release its heavenly tears, which in actuality is our own liberation within.

There is something else the body does as well. It gathers all the ominous experiences that have beset you, and when the pressure is too strong, these dark clouds then burst the boundaries of their own weight to cry upon the mountain peaks as a release of that which has accumulated.

As you know, the feelings that you ride upon reveal to you that the information these heavy raindrops bring to its majestic contours is a recognition of that which cannot be changed yet is transformed by simply letting go."

Master Turya looked at his disciples and assured them, "Nature understands our process, but can we recognize its reflection within this image presenting itself to us? It is a portrait being painted; we are just learning to recognize the hand of its artistry, through experience.

The mountain will essentially be teaching you timing. It will ask you, through all these lessons, to put aside your intellect and only journey with your feeling centers. These are the only eyes that can truly see. Tempering of one's spirit is the mountain's call to your own fortitude to stand up and notice it noticing you."

The Old Sage looked at the young devotees, "There is nothing personal within the predisposition of this terrain. This is one of the many lessons being revealed. In this way, I ask you to walk upon the footsteps of my memory.

Now, whether you have achieved your task or not, the night begins to call upon you.

In the first scenario, even though you have attained fire and shelter, your bones will still rattle in anticipation of the unexpected. As you know, when the night is closing in, it shields from you what you could previously see within the light of day—the predators that may surround you while you attempt to sleep.

The second situational consequence is more obvious. Your body will not only quiver, your whole *Being* will stir with fear welling up from within, for it knows it is in more danger now and may not survive the night. Darkness will hide the world from your view.

Fear can be detected. Panic rides upon the wind and calls predators to hunt the vulnerable. This is the teaching of the tiger claw.

The paw is no longer a comfort. Now, this soft cushion represents something else. This is a true collision factor, identifying safety and danger simultaneously. In other words, this is how a man becomes a mountain.

You must realize, my dear disciples, the omnipotence has surrounded us for an eternity. How can we travel toward what is already there? It is boundless.

Light only gives an impression that there is something to obtain. It measures the world in miles as we stand at the beginning of our path. Is not omnipresence more potent than light, when you consider this?

Yet, when you travel within, upon your eternal emptiness, light appears. Wordless realizations are unspoken sources of this reservoir. If we speak in reference to it, it gives us light. What a strange candle we are!"

Master Turya's words were brimming with wisdom. The men listened carefully as he continued.

"Similarly, when you walk through the rooms of your household in darkness, does it not follow you? Isn't it omnipresently available? I would ask you to ponder this, my loving disciples.

THE MOUNTAIN

Within your shelter, at the bottom of this majestic mountain, why do many things appear that you cannot see? What is the mountain teaching you when you have fire and shelter, in comparison to not having light and refuge?

For each one of you, the omnipresence reveals how to respond, in comparison to your internal fortitude.

Will your candle be snuffed out? Or will you have the general sensibility to accept what you cannot change and therefore change what is unacceptable? Is it within you, or is it outside of you?"

Seeing the faces of his disciples full of wonder, the Old Sage explained, "You have to understand, the omnipresence was already here before we arrived.

All sentient *Beings* that have self-reflective illumination will realize that the eternal emptiness is called upon to represent their light. My loving disciples, this may take a lifetime to come to terms with.

Is not the mountain wise? It is a reflection of your light being challenged. In essence, what I am now transmitting is that you are travelling toward what is already there. Isn't your destiny to add to the omnipresence within the limitations of your own light? This I wish you to ponder.

Deep inside this description of shelter and fire, or a lack of these two elements, what is this powerful mountain challenging you to realize? What is it really teaching us?

How did my Master, the mysterious Tibetan, transmit this omnipresence? And where did the words come from within me that you are now walking upon, deeply studying each step you take upon the cobblestones of your timeline? Your journey, my journey, the existence of all journeys, and every sentient *Being* within the vastness of our universes must come upon what I have just spoken.

As I look up into the sky, are not the stars a representation of our individual candles that wish to understand the omnipresence which upholds that light?"

The disciples were silent. The gravity of their Master's words touched them deeply. The kind and gentle Sage continued his discourse.

"In times past, the old world would show the marks of the land upon the wrinkles of one's face, revealing clearly what one has been through and survived. If one cannot endure these crevices within, the mountain will then swallow the man. So, it's best we have a few wrinkles, ah?" Master Turya looked affectionately at the men, as they all joined him in laughter.

"The next morning, you awaken upon a new world. For the first time you see what's in front of you. The ground is substantial, but there is still a possibility of you slipping on the gravel. Here is where you realize that timing is not something that can be measured by thought.

You see, my dear disciples, every step that is taken on your journey has within it both success and failure; thus, timing is an element of great interest. Your fate awaits you.

When you begin to climb a small ravine, which rock will you grab next? Is it anchored? Or is it loose enough for you to lose your grip? If you walk too soon on a narrow edge or walk too late, what is there waiting for you?

When you are too slow or too quick, will you place your hand or your foot in a spot which reveals a destiny that shows the fate of an ill-timed decision of the mind? Or will it be a perfectly-placed action of your body that is not possessed by thought?

There was an occasion in my life," the wise Sage recounted, "when I was walking and saw somebody noticing a turtle crossing a road. Its steps were sure and precise, and to that point, its timing was perfect.

This man ran to its aid, picked it up from the middle of the road, and placed it where he believed it would be safe. Ten hours later, as he returned from his journey, he discovered this sacred *Being* six more miles up the road. It had been flattened by a cart. The wooden wheels had crushed its shell.

Nobody in the old world would purposely kill such a *Being*. You have to realize this: the man holding the reins had turned his face to the left, smiling politely to a passerby and had not noticed the turtle there, beneath the wheel."

There was a deep silence again. The Old Sage's stories were bringing cascades of insights to the men listening in quiet absorption.

Turya looked up at his disciples and said, "The power of the turtle's timing was interfered with. If it had not been carried just a few feet away from its position, to a location which revealed danger, it would have prevailed, and it would still be alive.

Even though the turtle's timing was perfect, the man who picked it up from its path believed his actions were devoted to the perfection of his mindfulness. Thus, the mountain speaks to us in many different dialects.

It's easy to understand that if you are too soon or too late, your fate will reveal itself to you. The mountain has no mercy. There are no second chances; it is what it is. If you walk too quickly, you may fall into a deep ravine. If you wait too long, a tiger may pounce at you from behind. Either way, your life is taken. There is no luck; there is no tragedy. These are the eyes of the mountain. There's just *Is* and *Is not*.

As you reach your higher peaks and tentatively look back, be careful not to gather your previous moments; you know you can't bring the past with you. The complexity of your present timeline is all that matters. This will allow your steps to be firm and strong. In this portion of your journey, your heart becomes clear and powerful. Your eyes ascend to wisdom, just like the mountain you have diligently climbed.

As you come upon the full implications of your ascension, surrounded by cutting wind, the snow-covered ground reveals an enormous lake that has been fed by the icy peaks. You know deep within your bones you cannot look back to pull upon your past experiences to allow you to see what is to come next.

This is when you notice that a thunderstorm is holding the world still for a moment before it breaks. As you know, its rain represents renewal, a beginning, the commencement of a new journey. But, remember, at this crucial juncture it is imperative to pause—not to reach back and not to rush forward.

Realize this, my loving devotees, your past and future

are within your present moment. Is it not like walking? The foot that is behind you is pulled forward by the one in front, and is not your body the pendulum that reveals these two elements as one? There is an unseen complexity within our moments. Can you notice this?

Is our past not like jagged rocks? I will ask you to pick them up carefully and throw them into the deep waters that are presenting themselves to you. Let them be pulled by the gravity of the waterfall that is cascading from the lip of this mountain.

Realize, your memories are comprised of trials and tribulations that are harsh and unforgiving within their nature. But is it not this moment, this joyous point of transition, that will transcend what was into what will be?

You know that you need to be uninjured so that you have the capacity to grasp what is new without harm. The only alternative that you have at this point is to glance back and softly bid farewell to what you knew so as to embrace the unknown, new moments that are going to confront you.

Upon this crucial point of realization, you must take the jagged rocks of your previous experience and hurl them to the edge of these great still waters that reveal a massive cascade that is about to come upon you while journeying towards the flatlands, to the green fields and warm sunlight that will soon gently caress your face.

Here is where you firmly grasp the edge of the mountainous ravine, carefully descending. The massive waterfall that is beside you starts to reshape the cutting influence of your past as it plummets towards the rapids.

You have to be mindful, while steadily descending the first treacherous incline, to realize that these memories are no longer available visually to you. They have disappeared, consumed by the tumultuous waters.

Deep within your heart they are accompanying you, yet they are simultaneously within a transformational process, seemingly independent of your consciousness. Your past is neither late nor early. It arrives upon your moment in the balanced perfection of your future expression.

THE MOUNTAIN

The landscape of your present moment is as it is. It does not ask you for your past to accompany your steps. It simply observes who you are, not who you were. As each new circumstance arises, you realize the rapids have turned into swirling torrents. Your steps are now firmer; the waters have become clearer. Strangely enough, you can see that the memories which you have previously flung into this liquidity are now slowly transforming from what they were into what they are becoming. Your consciousness no longer has that previous jaggedness.

The days pass by, and the water follows you as you accompany it upon your shorelines. You glance once again into the still, clear water that is now your life. Reaching into this crystal-clear substance, you retrieve those stones that you once knew and can no longer identify, for now they are smooth, glistening from within, revealing the different contours and shapes of their colors as a renewed image of something unrecognizable.

They are you but don't resemble anything you expected. You are their *Not Doing*. Your past has no resemblance to your present existence. So from this perspective, how can you, at this point, reassemble the past?

My dear disciples, now that we have reached the flatlands and walk gently within the green fields of our future, as the sun caresses your face once again, this is not only the end but the beginning of your journey. It is time for you to take these polished stones of your experience and throw them into the middle of your mountain, so that they can be forgotten, yet remembered in a way that adapts in comparison to the reality of your present moment. In other words, these precious gems become a multifaceted diamond.

This is how the past becomes your future continuum that will seem unrecognizable yet reveals the beauty of what was into what is. This is the truest form of recapitulation. It leaves you exactly where you are, to review what presently arises, which brings us back to the mantra I gave you: *I am a Mountain, I AM.*

THE BODHI TREE

Seated at the side of their beloved Master, under the cool shade of the beautiful Bodhi tree, the disciples were looking forward to hearing more of his wisdom that touched their hearts so deeply. Acknowledging their respectful attention with an affectionate smile, the Wise Sage began.

"Now, it's time to ask me questions about your experiences that pertain to your memories, regarding the journey you have already taken.

We have not left the mango grove, yet we have moved from the base of the mountain to the precarious peaks and from there, made our way mindfully to the flatlands of new beginnings.

Be aware, you will travel upon my words that will become the mountain of your realizations. Embedded within these descriptions is the personal odyssey you will embark upon to decipher how they will shape your own awakening as I transmit to you what I know, which will equally alter your insights within our communion.

In other words, everything that I explain has multiple eddies woven within it. When your destiny meets mine, the seeds that awaken within you will inquire upon my journey as a profound revelation of your inwardly travelling steps.

Realize, there is much layered content within what I am passing on to you right now, and this will be revealed in nine different ways. It is therefore imperative that you give voice to what you come upon so as to make clear to yourselves what potential is hidden within my transmission.

Years ago, I spoke about the statue of Shiva that many villagers have in the altars of their homes. I did not describe two other elements that are presented within the symbolism of his dance—one of his right arms displays a cobra manifesting and in another, he is holding a rattle.

Now, I will combine these two elements into the reality of what is unseen, yet can be tangibly felt, which reveals itself deep within the interior of one's feeling center.

I have mentioned to you many times in the past that we have a lower gourd. Not only is this regulatory hub of internal power important to travel towards to realize our potential, it is essential that you become aware of the heart chakra, the second command center that is above this power point.

When these two combine harmoniously, in conjunction with the upper gourd of our balance center, many extraordinary things within become available by virtue of a mysterious cascade activating the dormant small chakras that lie deep inside one's physical framework. These are known as *Nadis*.

There are seventy-two thousand of them that work in correspondence with one hundred and fourteen chakras that spread throughout your physical form like the stars in the sky. They switch on and off, momentarily showing us our location within our connection to the *Akashic field* that we become awakened to in the emerging process of our *Being* coming upon the dance of life.

Shiva's right arm reveals a cobra coiling as ribbons of light around it to eventually appear underneath the palm of his hand. This represents the manifestation of the internal process of our lights awakening.

As this phenomenon awakens within us and travels through our hallways, we begin to vibrate. And when this reverberation finds consistent connection within the diversification of all the minute *nadis* and the major chakras moving in harmony, the physical eyes open to their inherent ability through the resonant field manifesting as visual components of sensory data that correspondingly inspire realizations, which the heart begins to recognize.

The rattle that Shiva holds in his left hand indicates internal frequencies manifesting within one's physical form as inaudible sound waves.

Now, as these secrets of his statue unveil themselves to us, I must open one more doorway for you to walk through, accompanied by your second feeling center so that you may experience what is necessary in order to irrefutably realize what is occurring."

The disciples were listening carefully as Master Turya was clearly illustrating to them things they had never before heard. Their eyes were smiling with anticipation as the Old Sage continued.

"This second regulatory center has magic hidden within it. This is how the *Unknown* transmits via my voice so that you can recognize the next part of Buddha's saying that I will again describe to you in its entirety, very soon."

Hearing his words, the men started laughing joyously, "Finally, Master, we don't have to wait!"

Smiling, the Old Sage said, *"Looking at what you can't see and feeling what cannot be touched, touches upon you to be seen* when you understand the next part of Buddha's scripture, which is *As others are, so am I.*

For one moment, I would like you to review your second regulatory center and realize it has revealed this wisdom to you all your life. The delicate hand of the *Unknown* reaches in and gracefully moves its fingers upon the inner breastplate of your chest, scanning the contours of your experiential realizations at the moment you feel them."

Hearing such an extraordinary explanation, one of the disciples asked, "Master, what are we looking for and have not noticed?"

"Look inside your heart right now," replied the Mango Grove Master. "Within the contours of its internal walls, there are slight protrusions that resemble raindrops falling through silk. While this gentle descent is occurring, the hand of eternity is reaching towards the acoustic pressure becoming available to its subtle dexterity and reading it as if it were braille.

As you ride upon these momentary contours, the subtle hand of wisdom absorbs your realizations of *Inaction* as a transmission. And while these delicate digits swiftly, with utmost precision, interpret these frequencies, this acoustic song is being sung within you as a prayer received.

At this point, we are no longer *As I am, so are others.* We have graduated to *As others are, so am I.*

Thus identifying the truth of this reality, we walk upon the revelations of our reflective mechanisms which in actuality are the empty hub of the holographic wheels turning within the eternal expression of themselves. This is how we connect to the diversification of our individual *Akashic wisdom.*

Identifying ourselves in comparison to this, we realize *nothing should be harmed.* Which brings us to the next part of Buddha's saying, *Harm no one, nor have them harmed.*"

THE RIDDLE

After some time in meditation under the Bodhi tree, the disciples and several villagers visiting the mango grove were all patiently waiting for the Sage to commence his discourse.

"Dear friends, the *Knowing and Doing* principle that I have introduced earlier within my teachings must now be disseminated so as to settle within your intellectuality before being grasped by your heart. This communication on *Knowings and Doings* has many elements hidden within it that we need to tease to the surface for examination.

I must warn you to be prepared. The descriptions I am about to impart may bring upon you what I wish to convey. It has nothing to do with us but with the historical nature of our *Knowings and Doings* not being seen for what they truly are. I am reticent to relay this knowledge, but it is necessary so as to uproot the weeds within the field of our prosperity.

The first component that we must look at is how our past gains unnecessary relevance through *Knowing and Doing* the forceful present moments of all the people in the world that are around us from birth.

The *Knowings and Doings* of the present are *Knowings and Doings* of the past, and both of these factors are contingent upon the bias that one has been brought up with. There is a present-moment-cultural *Knowing and Doing* and there are repetitive, reflective components of justifiable points embedded in memory.

A *Knowing* is when somebody believes they are certain about the realizations within their present moment in comparison to all they have learned up to that point—which in the long run justifies their opinion. This is always contingent on the reflexive memory and emotional stabilization of righteousness.

Here I am talking about world cultures within their diversity. Every country reflects their understanding in comparison to what presents itself as a challenge. This bias strengthens and simultaneously undermines through the prospect of intellectual discourse without the true mechanisms of the heart—even though one's heart can be involved in *Knowing and Doing*. That's why this subject is a profound riddle.

This struggle is expressed externally as overt gestures of domination from one individual to another. At the same moment, the battle is occurring internally, betwixt one's emotions and mind, which further solidifies the bias.

Knowing and Doing is also reinforced by discordant feelings like jealousy, anger, greed, resentment, and arrogance and is supported via the bow of one's internal intentions so as to release this disharmonious poison arrow amidst all circumstances that trigger its fundamental feeling of insecurity. In other words, *Knowing and Doing* is propelled by an unbalanced disposition.

These states of *Being* can implode within as internal tendencies manifesting as a stealth cloaked bandit within darkness preparing to establish distance from the circumstances, or like a sniper, covertly wreaking havoc so as not to be identified as the root of that disharmony.

Realize, this means tipping the internal scales of our observation towards the most destructive manifestations of *Knowings and Doings*. Is this not how wars begin amidst these wooden spokes?

At no point have we spoken about the true righteousness of the heart that can rise to defend its purity amidst this poverty. Within this reflection, we are mainly reviewing emotional eddies, which are actively applied towards what is seen as a threat to one's standpoint.

Remember, I mentioned that the donkey is smart, and this cannot be underestimated or overlooked. If it is, great conflict may arise. If history is not heeded, it is destined to repeat itself, from a micro to macrocosmic level which is expressed from personal to worldwide perspectives.

Visiting all these relevant points is nothing but a rehash of what is being brought from the past to the present so repetitively that it is difficult to notice one's bias when this occurs.

In actuality, every moment that exists as a *Knowing and a Doing* is nothing more than repetition given the mantle of intelligence through the standpoints being practiced and integrated into a unified front.

Whether it can be seen or not, this has to do with opportunities lost, filling those chasms of emotional deficits, and bringing them into the forefront to look like strength, when in actuality there is nothing more than a petty dictatorship, born of the moral dilemmas arising from within, attempting to assert itself.

The only way to understand how to dismantle these bindings is to ask each individual that is *Knowing and Doing* to review their present moment resistances as nothing more than dysfunctional feelings from the past, presenting themselves as a selective justification of subjectivity that defends a deep-seated emotional viewpoint. This must be recognized.

See it this way: The temperamental eddies that are frequencies pass their discordance from person to person generationally, thus not being noticed. When this transfer occurs, it must be recognized as a form of rational insanity, attempting to change the cogs of a wheel with new ones, which is nothing but repetition. The internal mechanism will function in exactly the same way, even though it has been replaced.

Knowing and Doing can be categorized as one state of consciousness confirming itself over and over again. This repetitive tendency must be informed about *Not Doing* so as to witness the illusion of subjective bias from a renewed standpoint of non-involvement. Before we go any further with these concepts, do you have any questions?"

"Master, over the years, you've taught us through strong example and powerful metaphor, and this is the reason why I have attempted to look for all the secrets of your actions within my own doings.

Righteousness, as I understand it, is a latent, innate frequency that belongs to one's belt, like the machete. It guards and protects the integrity of the physical *Being*, in the sense of being guided by the right feeling inside when some external phenomenon attempts to trigger one into something.

But I have noticed that via interference, it can also become an instrument of self-justification to sustain a *Knowing and Doing*. Is there a way to differentiate between these two positions?"

"My dear disciple, your mind is searching for me, locating all the areas of your previous experiences within the mango grove from childhood until now. What is being revealed through your question is your expansiveness toward situational awareness becoming attunement.

Your machete has a purpose, but I have never mentioned anything about your belt. As I travel upon your conclusions, I realize that you are asking the world to reveal its prayer to you. This within itself is a *siddhi*, a power that can accompany you through the awakening force of a *nadi* becoming available—a small chakra that shines its light upon an epiphany which relates to the substance of the belt and the *nadi* simultaneously.

Yet, remember, a *siddhi* has only two possibilities contained within it: imprisonment or freedom, motive or no motive. But I will further explain this in the future.

Everything within our reality is a tapestry, and this is the woven individuality of a thread. Realize, what I am doing right now is pictorial in nature. I am describing a carpet that has been masterfully put together by a weaver. The voice of the empty hub reveals these threads as what they truly are—magical singularities that will express themselves through the inner nature of the one who recognizes them.

Now, let me take you back to your path. Know that we are flying on this carpet. I wish to show you one more thread within this complex time-space continuum that is our linear timeline revealing the intricacy of these old teachings."

All the gathered disciples and guests were sitting down, quietly watching the Mango Grove Master as he spoke.

THE RIDDLE

"Remember, I mentioned to you in the past that we have different facial features as well as length of bones and that the general shape of our body by itself will produce its own unique frequencies or realizations.

What I am saying is the manifestation of the belt has now become your metaphor. The *Unknown* speaks in mysterious ways and will only appear if one has no motive. And at the moment this discourse is about *Knowing and Doing*, which is disharmonious causality manifesting. Even if it seems rational, it really is not.

Remember, it takes ten thousand swords of *Inaction* to defeat one blade of *Knowing and Doing*. This leads us towards the caduceus principle—which is about finding balance—combined with the Medusa complex, which represents the diverse elements of trickery that spring from the mind, as depicted in the image of one hundred snakes arising as her hair.

Once again, this is your riddle to be revealed to yourself in the full complexities of your *Inactions*, reviewing who you are, for yourself and everybody else simultaneously.

THE RIDDLE

Realize, the tone of my voice has changed. What I am doing right now is putting everything of relevance in front of your discernment, with its own weight as a planetary force. In other words, I am no longer giving you small pieces at once. Not to confuse anyone here under the Bodhi tree, but to challenge you individually to come upon yourselves through these complexities.

Be clear. Understand that these teachings are like a magical carpet. And are you all not the threads that are revealing its pattern—either to walk on as a *Doing* or to fly upon as a *Not Doing*? Realize, the next subject and the subject beyond that, and so on and so forth, are contained within the whole, even though we are looking at one thread at this moment.

Nevertheless, let's continue with more questions about this preliminary subject of *Knowing and Doing*, which in actuality, my dear disciples, is the sour fruit."

"Master, can you please speak about situational awareness becoming attunement? What do you mean by this?"

"Situational awareness is the physical manifestation of the world around you. For someone to be conscious like this, they must become internally physically attuned. Yet, one's vibratory perception can be corrupted by personal bias. If situational awareness does not judge but knows what it sees, there is more likelihood of a pure attunement consciousness appearing. Obviously, it will have subtle *Knowings* inside of it, but the variables are immense in comparison to *homeostasis*—the rigid reality of *Doing!*"

"Master, in the beginning, do *Not Doings* have *Doings* hidden within them?"

"The *Doings* within *Not Doings* are like flakes of snow falling onto hot stones. They simply cannot withstand the fires of one's heart, which immediately transforms one frequency into another through *Inaction* that transmutes the original bias within the devotional act of service.

It is the same as one's breath. You breathe in oxygen and exhale carbon dioxide. There is no time when one element isn't affected by the other. It is how we travel upon the variables that will uphold the continuity of our thresholds, always delivering to us their enlightenment.

To emphasize, we must sustain at all times a stance of non-interference. Yet, in the very same breath, we are aware of all the resistant components within the arising possibilities of perception. That also brings *Not Doing* into question, not via the mind but contained inside the subtle equations that arise within nuances of discernment that will always have the principle of *do no harm* underpinning them."

"Master, can you explain more about the change in the tone of your voice?"

"If you noticed a shift in my discourse, there are only two possibilities: a micro-gesture of emotional influence or the true internal realization of one's heart process arising. But remember, this is complex—it is the *Passerby* principle. Do you realize, or do you really realize? This is your riddle to undo."

"Master, can you give us an example of how a *siddhi* can become imprisonment or freedom? Why is it important at this stage not to have motive?"

"To operate without expectation is important at every point of realization within one's *Being*. There are only two subtle variables of influx: your motive to do something or the world requesting you to notice. More than likely, it is asking for your acknowledgment. And in this case, you will reciprocate without knowing why. However, if you do know why you are acting in response to the world, that is your motive.

Being nobody is tricky. Convincing everybody that you are somebody, by appearing to be nobody, is deception. Be careful. This is the fox stealing our hens in the middle of the night while we are sleeping. As you can see, corruption has many variables. This harkens back to the hundred snakes on Medusa's head. But now let's take a look at the principle of *Morphogenesis*."

MORPHOGENESIS

With a generous smile, the Old Sage took a moment to acknowledge the sincere attention of all the participants in the mango grove.

"At this point, *Knowing* one's *Doings* is revealing how this first principle has ordered itself in a form of *homeostasis*. All elements are organized in comparison to the localized items of one's familiar environment.

As you know, in our solar system, many planets revolve around our sun. The planetary force of all the containment fields of each heavenly body has in it a frequency that emanates from its core and inevitably affects our consciousness as a humanity. These nine revolving orbs reveal different levels of acoustic pulsations.

We are affected via these variables from each planet. And it is this attunement that causes a destabilization that is necessary for our species' development. We will look at this phenomenon and call it *morphogenesis*.

Though these terms may seem radical in comparison to the language I have used previously, it is important for you to grasp these concepts, as *Knowing and Doing* is nothing more than *homeostasis*, while *Not Doing* is an expression of *morphogenesis*.

This form of semantics that I am revealing at the moment relates to biological predispositions which we are going to examine in the same manner that a mechanic would pull an engine apart. We will remove every single item, in an orderly way, from the beginning to the end, which is disassembling, and from the end to the beginning, which is reverse-engineering.

Once a specialist understands this process, all they need

to do is to listen to the engine when it is operational. From that point on, he can detect a slight variance within the mechanisms of that which he is traveling into, through applying his listening power as a diagnostic tool.

The mechanic will use his eyes, ears, and feeling centers in such a way that he *becomes* the engine. So we can fully see that our biological predisposition is to acquire, through our listening power towards our internal engine, logical conclusions that emerge from our bodily intelligence, not the mind.

What I am suggesting is that we have overlooked this innate ability of our own biology that is transporting us through life. *Knowing and Doing* reveals its function when something breaks down. But, unlike an engine, human beings are governed by software not hardware.

It is our solemn duty as sentient *Beings* to reverse-engineer this process of *Knowing and Doing* and discover where these nine variables of our planetary system are being harnessed within our situational awareness in order to evolve beyond this to a state of attunement.

Firstly, we must look at the most solidified component of our physicality and then move on to the *Being* travelling within this vessel, which can be seen as an energy body or a transdimensional awareness. For as we know, our physicality and spiritual endeavors are intimately connected.

The second thing we must examine very carefully is how to transmute *Knowing and Doing*, and discover why this is necessary for our own personal evolutionary process.

We are a *Human Being* that is *Knowing and Doing*. Here we have to open up the first possibility of transformation and ask a very serious question: What does *Human Being* really mean? Through *Knowing and Doing* we cannot discover this.

Here is our first challenge. We can't change the fact that we are a *Human Being*, but we can change our *Doings* into something other than what they are so as to open up a form of neutrality within our *Beingness*. This can be achieved by *Not Doing* our *Doings*. Let's consider this thoroughly, in a step-by-step approach.

Imagine that you are standing in a room full of people.

They all individually come to shake your hand to introduce themselves. On the level of your physiology, you are confronted with their frequencies, and within their physical predispositions you are noticing micro-gestures, whether they be grossly manifesting or subtly revealing their nature.

There is a preemptive force within *Knowing and Doing* which is very valuable for one's primal survival. Once a *Human Being* has learned to identify a mannerism through repetition, *Knowing* and *Doing* will automatically *Do* that *Knowing* for them.

This spontaneously falls under a structural bias that is absolutely true for the one witnessing it. It is an irrefutable *Knowing* that must not be ignored. But it is what you *Do* with it next that is more important. You understand now why I have asked you all these years to notice and not judge—yet *Know* undeniably what you have seen.

This is where we come upon the deeper aspects of the original riddle of *Knowing and Doing*. The person that we are observing is travelling upon their waters. You, too, can see yourself in exactly the same fashion. Now, we must see

Knowing and Doing through the lens of this description.

Once you realize what you recognize, a part of this *Knowing* is like a crane that picks up the cargo of the ship you are observing and transports the container of your realizations onto your own vessel. You are *Knowing and Doing* your situational awareness into your feeling center of attunement. The level of frequency that you absorb is obviously contingent upon your bias of perception.

Each vessel has a rudder, and this directs your ship of awareness, thus affecting what you become conscious of. The rivers of our lives are moved in waves of realizations. In terms of interaction, this will have an effect on both parties, whether we like it or not.

What I am saying is that the stability of our waters is contingent on the external environment, which is either calm or tumultuous. In other words, storms may cause a disruption to our sea of perception.

Hopefully, this is enough clarification to allow you all to understand that *Being, Knowing, and Doing* is like the wooden spokes in the waters of our consciousness. We can't ignore what we know, but it is what we *Do* and *Don't Do* with what we notice that is of outmost importance.

I am going to ask you *Not to Do* what you know. Whatever you believe you have discovered about another person, pause, and do not exchange your bias for another *Doing*. Transform it into a *Not Doing*.

And the way that this is done is to allow yourself to notice what you are doing with your *Doing* before you are asked *Not to Do* it. This is your initial task, which is *Not Doing* somebody else first. This prompts you to simultaneously *Not Do* yourself.

What I mean by this is to identify and arrest the second level of discourse that you are going to have with yourself. Remember, I am still talking about *Knowing and Doing,* and have asked you to exchange this with *Not Doing* yourself so that this will become your discipline, your devotion, not only to the person you have identified but to yourself simultaneously.

If you're *Doing* a person via your realization of their presentation towards you, I would ask you to humbly put your eyes down and simply disengage from those *Knowings*.

Now, sincerely look within yourself and begin to notice that you are using your emotional predisposition to instigate the process of having a discussion with yourself, privately, about that person. This is the second level of *Knowing and Doing* that you must prevent from occurring.

The emotion that you have represents another person within you that you want to have a conversation with from the standpoint of your mind. When you notice this clearly, it will loop over and over again in terms of a loaded, repetitive mental process talking to itself—rationalizing the emotion to the mind then the mind to the emotion, stabilizing its own repetition so as to verify to yourself that you are right.

This in essence is your *thief* and *ghost* that you have noticed, and these two phenomena are interchangeable in comparison to motive, which leads back to your emotional predisposition that you have not resolved. And this has to be recognized as a four-way exchange between two people.

The *ghost* is your emotional tendency that becomes the mind *thief*. These two elements are switchable between two people and are alchemically exchanged. This is your first recognition of how gossip from within manifests.

We are still *Knowing and Doing* right now. Even though I have requested you to lower your eyes and bring a downward gaze, I would ask you to look back up at the person, metaphorically speaking.

Realize that their threat to your stability is their *thief* that has projected from itself their *ghost* through micro-gestures to your body to activate your own *ghost*—which alerts your *thief*.

This interaction then becomes a perpetual loop of weaponized situational awareness and attunement combined into an eddy of repetition within the waters of perception. This you must halt through *Not Doing* your emotional reactivity toward the presentation of what you *Know*, which in actuality is valid to a certain point.

So if your *Knowing* is a *thief* and your internal reaction is your *ghost*, it is now your responsibility to reassemble these into a *Not Doing*.

Firstly, do not worry about your realizations in terms of *Knowing*. Look at your emotional reactivity: if it is there, then you have a *ghost*. If your internal *thief* gossips about this, you have discovered your mind. Your emotions are your *ghost* and your mind is your *thief*—rearranging the emotions to suit its motive. These two are symbiotically cooperating. Very simple, isn't it?" asked the Master, smiling generously at the visitors who had come to accompany him underneath the Bodhi tree.

"Here is where we change this internal interactivity into a structured form of *morphogenesis* that is illuminated by your *Inactions*. You initially must *Not Do* the emotional disruption, and, correspondingly, you cannot entertain thoughts as a supportive mechanism towards this process.

The first technique I will add here is very simple and will transform your reality. Instead of thinking your thoughts, breathe them deeply into your belly and release them through your outward breath. This is how breath overtakes the mind, and this will represent one of your first *Not Doings*.

Now, we must go to the next level of understanding this process and how everybody turns this internal *Knowing and Doing* into their external drama. For instance, you've noticed something about somebody. You do not like it and are going to take your own *thief* and *ghost* and talk to your best friend about that person. I must remind you now that we are in the area of *Harm no one*—which is, in actuality, yourself—*nor have them harmed*—which represents somebody else.

In other words, you have an emotional predisposition, which is your *ghost*, and you want to transfer this self-righteousness to another human being. You are the *thief* at this point, searching within the chambers of another *being* so you can activate their *thief* mechanism through your discourse of interactivity—or, plainly stated, gossip—to reinforce your righteousness.

Even though I have explained extensively about *Knowing and Doing*, here I am showing you what you need *Not to Do* to discover how to come upon your own neutrality, your inner *Beingness*, as the first step towards your own *divine nature.*

Without this *Inaction* occurring, it is difficult for a human being to discover the most sought-after realization within their sentience: *No Place, Emptiness, the Eternal Tao.* And the only way to get there is to discover your own neutrality.

You see, my loving disciples, *No Place*—the face of *Emptiness*—is far removed from our rudimentary status as human beings. In reality, it has its own neutrality. We will speak about this in the future.

First, you have to identify the neutral point within your *Beingness* and learn to graduate your own resistances and bias through this process of *Not Doing* all those learned aspects which you must turn incrementally into *Not Doings.*

Even though we are talking about *Not Doing* as our priority within this discourse, the focus is still on *Doing*. Now the emphasis will be upon your soft *Inaction*, which is to look very carefully at where graduation occurs in between *Doing* and *Not Doing* yourself.

In other words, my dear friends, by *Not Doing* other people you learn the discipline of simultaneously *Not Doing* yourself."

"Master, when we identify a *ghost* as the representation of an emotion transferred from somebody else's *thief*, how can we better cope with it? Also, how can we stop our own *thief* from sending its *ghost* to somebody else?"

"As you are a novice to the principles that I have taught the disciples in the mango grove, I will answer your question in the way that you have inquired. There is an admission within the micro-gestures of your words spoken, which openly reveals that you have a *ghost* and a *thief* operational, so this requires me to respond directly to that communication in the same vein.

Firstly, you don't *Do* that person—by not having your own thought process coupled with an emotional bias towards their *Being* active within you. This is the *Not Doing* part of it. Once you are becoming familiar with the process of stopping your reactive thoughts and emotions, you then come upon your humble observation of that individual, thus *doing no harm.*

The next step is to respectfully witness the feelings that call you to notice the transformation of the discord into something to meditate upon. Now, the way this occurs is obviously not to talk to yourself, nor entertain any discordant feelings about what has happened. This becomes your meditation which then transforms into an act of service to your environment through hard work or devotional supportiveness to those you love.

This requires you to *be your simple, beautiful self* without any form of attachment toward the people around you which may reveal your motive. If expectation is there, it's not an act of devotion nor a meditation."

"Master, what does the *four-way exchange between two people* mean?"

"The four-way exchange is a complex interplay between two individuals' minds and emotions that engages reflexive mechanisms which feed into their respective biases, whether it be via conflict or cooperation."

"Master, can you speak more about graduation between *Doing* and *Not Doing* oneself and how this is experienced in terms of feeling?"

"The way graduation occurs is that when you don't *Do* another person and you don't *Do* yourself, a very subtle frequency appears. You must realize, this delicate sound wave has been hijacked by a socially-engineered bias. The outer layer of subjectivity is denser in comparison to the original acoustics, and we lose our ability to detect them via this overload. I will explain more about this when we speak about the *Passerby* principle.

"Master, from your answer to a previous question, I realized there is also a soft difference in between *Don't Do* a person and *Not Do* them, in the sense that the first part is a slight *Doing*, that is, diligently applying a continual process of self-regulation based on situational awareness, while *Not Doing* them has become an automated process of attunement to *Harm no one, nor have them harmed*. Is this also a type of graduation?"

"Yes, indeed, this is. What you are experiencing is a

tender dexterity of the *Unknown* becoming tangible within your heart. The expansiveness within this awareness is unlimited, and it is fully contingent on your capacity to be humbled by the fact that your physical form will not be here very long.

We are limited in this way for very good reason. Our death whispers its subtleties of harmony to us, gently saying in our ear: *There is not much time.*

Even though I haven't mentioned this, I have experienced many variables in terms of timelines, which actually means I had contact with my other lifetimes within glimpses, yet the eternal process of my essential capacity to live reminds me constantly that I will die. If one would live until the age of ninety, five times ninety is four hundred and fifty years, yet, with this power of time behind my words, I still recognize there is no time to be wasted.

There are many different types of convergences, even within only one lifetime. There are thousands of years that can be grasped within one. You just need to know what to *Do* with your *Not Doings* when this occurs. My devoted disciple, you have discovered one of these keys. It has revealed itself to you in that subtle resonance you mentioned, and it is this frequency that I ride upon as your Master, to discover all the variables that are hidden within the voice of my heart. Here is where we find our true continual knot—a never-ending influx of awakening.

"Master, can you please tell us more about how one can replace thinking with breathing?"

"As you focus on your breath, your hearing, seeing, and feeling power follow the subtle nature of breathing into the abdomen, where stillness can be observed within its exact center, bypassing the resistances of the mind through this observation."

"Master, what happens to the *ghost* if the mind is stopped?

"It never existed in the first place. You go back to your original nature of thoughtlessness. This is how your listening power arises from within so as to allow the *Akashic field* to be spoken. It is the exact opposite to the thought process which has a fundamental tendency to forestall the heart's ability to rise to the occasion or to fulfill its true expression.

This is exactly the same as the explanation I gave to you years ago: When you reach for a glass of water, the mind said it did it where in actuality, the body started it."

"Master, how is human neutrality different from *No Place* neutrality?"

"There are fundamental similarities between the neutrality of *No Place* and the unbiased view of human perception. They both have frequencies emanating from a neutral point.

The only way to graduate to the neutral sphere of *No Place* is to wait patiently for one's bias to disappear. In between *Doing* and *Not Doing*, one must diligently pause, in a state of devotion, until wisdom arises of its own accord, thus allowing the heart to speak on one's behalf.

The heart can be seen as the empty hub of our humanness. The emptiness of *No Place* is expressed through a field of neutrality that is very difficult to discover via the

Knowings and Doings that are lodged within human attention.

To come upon this, we must die to every moment that asks us to realize the transition between life and death, or live with the prospect of death within our life.

If anything, what I am doing with the expression of this philosophy is to prepare you for the inevitability that is your unalterable journey into emptiness.

Look at it this way: *In the end we are the sum total of our doings and we will be faced by those doings at the moment of our death. Or is it our death in every moment that we live that faces us with what we do?*

Ponder this very carefully. The reason we have to be naked, in this crucial moment of change from something to nothing, is of vital emphasis to understand. The point is to take as little as possible into this sphere of awareness. When you die, you will realize that the less you carry of yourself, the easier the transition will be.

If a person is faced with death without having discipline, the Unknown can be more than shocking, and the challenges can be extremely untenable, in many cases horrifying.

Realize that these horrors are just a test to see if you have the possibility to let go of what is presenting itself to you. This transitional Bardo is simply asking you to *Not Do* the nightmare that you have brought with you. Now you can see how life can be a preparation for death.

Since you have asked me this question, I will give you one more technique to strengthen your ability to stay clear for those days in limbo before the decision is made for you, or where you can make that decision for yourself.

The technique is: When you fall asleep at night, become aware of the transition from wakefulness to sleeping. Is this not Bardo? Do not seek out dreams for they will, in turn, seek you. Dreaming is rudimentary. It is not advanced; it is basic. Having no form, thoughts, or visions within one's dreams is of a higher consciousness. Why would anyone bother intentionally dreaming when emptiness is the goal? Is that not a repetition of waking?

Just sleeping is *Not Doing* dreaming. But the *Doing* of

dreaming has to be empty of itself. The *Not Doing* of waking is *Not to Do* it. In other words, emptiness is within light, and is not light within darkness?" the Mango Grove Master asked them, chuckling gently.

"Master, how do the *ghost* and the *thief* elementally exchange between themselves? What do you mean by that?"

"The mind and emotions take favored portions of each other to expand upon their own stupidity," said the Master, laughing. "Remember, I told you years ago that the mind is an ass, an odious element of the wooden spokes."

"Master, I understand how situational awareness can become weaponized via the repetitive transferal of *ghosts* and *thieves* between people, but how can attunement become so?"

"Attunement basically means a frequency is exchanged via resonance. If negatively directed, it becomes a destructive *Doing*. Then there is the subtle attunement of *Not Doing* that expression that arises from within to be witnessed if one's internal quietude is profound."

"Master, is *Not Doing* an expression of *morphogenesis*? Is there a morphing part and a generating part coming about as a result of applying this principle?"

"*Not Doing* is something that can't be rationally explained in terms of *morphogenesis*. This you will have to wait for so that your own intelligence can see itself arising without your influence."

MISPLACED MEMORIES

PART ONE

"Master, can you explain how our memory works, and how we can cope with the bias within it? And where is that *Doing* in our prejudice?

I remember years ago you said: *You cannot trust your recollections; you can only examine who you are in the moment that arises.* Can you please say more, so that we can find clarity within this elusive subject? I recall you also mentioned that *time is continually escaping us and within this we are perpetually being renewed.*"

"My dear disciples, our future and past are very much

contingent on our present moment. These three states are in constant flux, and we must diligently move to the center of our internal quietude so as not to be drawn into their bias.

Our present moments habitually rely on our *Knowings and Doings*. Our past is contingent upon our memory of all of the *Doings* that brought us into our current position. Realize, though, this is highly selective. *Not Doing* will rearrange the *Knowings* into their elusive, fluid equilibrium, which is a transitional point of awareness flowing from emptiness into the creation of something that is never driven by willful desire.

Motive, in essence, is the greatest enemy that has ever challenged us. There are so many ways to look at this, within its complexity. We are going to examine the implications of consciousness being mismanaged, to bring clarity to memories that seem clear, yet are clouded.

I will now relay a story to you that will identify the nature of this fog. I would like to transport you within your visual imagery as you follow my words, thus giving you a memory that is a mere example of how recall can be misappropriated.

There was a young boy who lived alone with his mother in a hut, in a small village in India. She would often say in a tender tone that contained no form of accusation, 'I wish your father was here with us.' As the years rolled by, her son came to feel extremely disenfranchised because of his absence.

Around the age of ten, his dad reappeared without explanation. He was full of promises, hopes, and dreams, stating to the young boy that he had changed, that he would be present in his life from this point onwards—thereby admitting that his absence was not right—and that he was very sorry for not being there.

You must realize, my beloved disciples, that the child, at this stage, was very emotionally charged and was prepared to forgive his father if the merits of his actions were enough to quell the fire of his resentments."

Pausing for a moment, the Master of the Mango Grove asked, "Is that not motive, one of the most destructive *Doings* that we have in our perception? Remember the philosophy of the *thief* and the *ghost*? Can you see how it is now being fed into this circumstance? The question is: Does the father have the discipline to achieve what he has promised? Let us continue.

Being aware of his child's predisposition, the father knew he had to build upon his good deeds within the eyes of his son so as to be forgiven.

'Let's do something together,' he proclaimed. 'My brother has a hut in the jungle. Let's go there to spend some time, so we can go fishing and play catch, climb coconut trees—all the things we should have done but have not yet.'

Saying this, he noticed his son's dog jumping up and down in excitement. Picking up his ball, the father threw it across the yard, and they both smiled, seeing him scrambling feverishly to fetch it. 'Let's take Doodly with us,' he suggested.

Hearing this, the young boy was delighted and happily exclaimed, 'Fantastic, Dad, that sounds great!'

'Ok! I'll pick you up tomorrow at ten so we can ride to the hut.'

The next morning, the boy was patiently waiting at his door step with Doodly sitting by his side. An hour went by, and his father had not arrived. Believing that his dad was breaking his promise, he was about to walk back inside when he heard him approaching.

'Hee-haw, hee-haw,' announced the donkey. Once in front of the boy's home, his dad jumped out of the cart and said, 'Sorry I'm late. I slept in. Let's get on the road.'

The young boy jumped up enthusiastically, forgetting all of the disappointment that he had previously felt. Running towards the cart in excitement, he threw his things in the back, calling out to Doodly to sit with him.

'Make yourself comfortable,' his father said, 'We have a six-and-a-half-hour ride till we reach the hut. We will be there just before nightfall,' he added smiling. Two hours into the journey, the young boy noticed a strange odor. 'Dad, what's that smell?'

'Oh, don't worry, son. It's just the donkey, farting. He ate too much sweet clover this morning, and it gave him bad wind.'

In a jovial tone, the boy complained, 'Oh, no! Four more hours of a farting ass.'

Laughing uproariously, his father said to him, 'You know, donkeys are very smart. On a trail of a thousand miles, if they put their hoof in a hole, regardless of where it is located, they will never step in that indentation ever again, no matter how many times they walk that path. And for us, this is very lucky. Because when this happens, they accidentally break wind,' he added, and they laughed joyously together, as they rumbled along the jungle path.

Travelling through a nearby village, about an hour before reaching the hut, he said to his son, 'We'd best grab some chaat for us and some chicken wings for Doodly from this roadside vendor because we have no food waiting for us at the hut.'

The long trip passed in the blink of an eye, and they

promptly arrived upon the jungle abode. It was a wonderful property, with large leaf-bearing trees and a beautiful river.

'Let's settle in, before it gets dark,' said the boy's father.

The accommodation was very basic but extremely comfortable. He proceeded to light a kerosene lamp so they could fall asleep witnessing the soft, yellow hue within the room.

'Wake me up at five-thirty,' he said, 'so we can go fishing, play catch with Doodly, and climb the nearby coconut tree to have fresh water to drink from its seed.'

The night slipped by very quickly. The young boy awoke just before dawn and gently shook his father's shoulder.

'Dad, wake up. It's time to get up.' His father mumbled, 'Give me a while longer. I'll be up soon.' The boy waited for half an hour before trying again to wake his father, repeatedly shaking his shoulder and saying, 'Dad, it is time to get up.'

The second time around, the boy started to become frustrated and annoyed. Sitting down abruptly on the front step of the hut, he found himself reimagining the feelings of disappointment that had haunted him previously. Infused with this mood, he stood up impatiently and went to his father's side, shaking his shoulder more vigorously, 'Dad, you promised you would wake up.'

Grumbling once again, his father said, 'Give me a few more minutes. I'm very tired.' At this point, the boy became infuriated. He stomped outside and sat on a nearby tree trunk with a cloud of animosity surrounding him. This time he did not go back in half an hour to wake his father up. He sat there, allowing the feelings of disappointment and anger to boil inside of him.

It was now close to midday. He went back to the hut to see where his father was and noticed that he was sitting up, holding his head in his hands, 'Oh, my gosh, what time is it?' he asked.

'It is almost twelve,' the boy answered flatly.

'I'm sorry! We've missed the early morning fishing,' said his father, 'and my brother doesn't have a raft to go out into the deeper waters where they are now. We'd better get the donkey and cart and travel back into the village so we have some food to eat tonight. Call Doodly, and we can go fishing tomorrow.'

Arriving back at the hut, they sat down and once again had a meal the same way they did the night before.

'We didn't fish, we didn't play ball, and we haven't climbed the coconut tree,' the boy stated in a sullen tone.

'I really apologize,' the father said. 'Please, forgive me. We'll do it tomorrow. Now, it is probably best that we go collect some wood for the evening fire so that we can enjoy each other's company in the light of the dancing flames. The young boy agreed, 'Ok, Dad, let's do that.'

Looking straight into his son's young, eager eyes, the father gently put his heavy palm on his shoulder, saying, 'Would you mind doing this for me, as I need some moments to recover. I feel so tired. I'll see you when this is done.'

When the young boy had collected the appropriate amount of wood for the evening, he noticed his father was sleeping already. Throwing the kindling down violently, he stomped loudly through the room and lay down on his bed, full of resentment and deep-seated animosity.

The next morning, as the sun was arising, the boy got up and shook his father's shoulder again. Just like the day before, he grumbled, 'Please give me half an hour more. I am so tired.'

The boy, at this stage, became enraged that the whole scenario was being repeated again. He decided, though, he wouldn't go back to wake his father the second or the third time. Instead, he sat on the front step of the hut, contemplating how furious he would be by the time his father woke up.

When his dad did finally arise, it was one-o'clock in the afternoon. Bleary-eyed, he asked, 'Oh, what time is it?'

The boy stood up and angrily said to him, 'It's too late for fishing. The morning catch is no longer near the shore. They have already migrated to the center of the river, and we have no canoe. We have not played ball, nor have we climbed the coconut tree. I have been waiting outside of the hut for hours,' the boy complained. 'Now we have no food, no water, and it is obvious we have to get the donkey and the cart to go into the small village and waste another two hours going back and forth to fetch food for ourselves, instead of doing what you've promised.'

The father was going to tell his son something, but his son was so infuriated, he did not let him say a word. 'Let's go and get the food from the vendor, Dad. Otherwise we won't get back before it's dark.'"

MISPLACED MEMORIES

PART TWO

"My loving disciples, let us now return to the young boy's house and start this story right from the very beginning. Here is where I will repeat this tale with a slight variation so that you may realize something about memory.

There was a young boy who lived alone with his mother in a hut, in a small village in India. She would often say in a tender tone that contained no form of accusation, 'I wish your father was here with us.' As the years rolled by, her son came to feel extremely disenfranchised because of his absence.

Around the age of ten, his dad reappeared without explanation. He was full of promises, hopes, and dreams, stating to the young boy that he had changed, that he would now be present in his life from this point onwards—thereby admitting that his absence was not right—and that he was very sorry for not being there.

Being aware of his child's predisposition, the father knew he had to build upon his good deeds within the eyes of his son so as to be forgiven.

'Let's do something together,' he proclaimed. 'Your uncle has a hut in the jungle. Let's go there to spend some time so we can go fishing and play catch, climb coconut trees—all the things we should have done but have not yet.'

Saying this, he noticed his son's dog jumping up and down in excitement. Picking up his ball, the father threw it across the yard, and they both smiled, seeing him scrambling feverishly to fetch it. 'Let's take Doodly with us,' he suggested.

Hearing this, the young boy was delighted and happily

exclaimed, 'Fantastic, Dad, that sounds great!'

'Ok! I'll pick you up tomorrow at ten so we can ride to the hut.'

The next morning, the boy was patiently sitting on his front door step, with his arms affectionately wrapped around Doodly's neck. An hour went by and his father had not arrived. Believing that his dad was breaking his promise, he was about to stand up and walk back inside when he heard him approaching.

'Hee-haw, hee-haw,' the donkey announced. Once in front of the boy's home, his dad jumped out of the cart and said, 'Sorry I'm late. I slept in. Let's get on the road.'

The young boy stood up enthusiastically, forgetting all of the disappointment that he had previously felt. Running towards the cart in excitement, he threw his things in the back, calling out to Doodly to sit with him.

'Make yourself comfortable,' his father said, 'We have a six-and-a-half-hour ride till we reach the hut. We will be there just before dusk,' he added, smiling.

Two hours into the journey, the young boy noticed a strange odor. 'Dad, what's that smell?'

'Oh, don't worry, son. It's just the donkey, farting. He ate too much sweet clover this morning, and it gave him bad wind.'

In a jovial tone, the boy complained, 'Oh, no! Four more hours of a farting ass.'

Upon their moment of mirth, the donkey looked back towards them, bearing his teeth and lifting his tail as if threatening to continue his odious behavior.

Laughing uproariously, his father said to him, 'You know, donkeys are very smart. On a trail of a thousand miles, if they put their hoof in a hole, regardless of where it is located, they will never step in that indentation ever again, no matter how many times they repeat that journey. And for us, this is very lucky. Because when this happens, they accidentally break wind,' he added, and they laughed joyously together as their cart rumbled along the jungle path.

Travelling through a nearby village, about an hour

before reaching the hut, he said to his son, 'We'd best grab some chaat for us and some chicken wings for your dog from this roadside vendor because we have no food waiting for us at the hut.'

The long trip passed in the blink of an eye, and they promptly arrived upon the jungle abode. It was a wonderful property, with large leaf-bearing trees and a beautiful river.

'Let's settle in, before it gets dark,' said the boy's father.

The accommodation was very basic but extremely comfortable. He proceeded to light a kerosene lamp so they could fall asleep witnessing the soft, yellow hue within the room.

'Wake me up early in the morning,' he said, 'so we can go fishing, play catch with Doodly and climb the nearby coconut tree to collect fresh water from its seed.'

The night slipped by very quickly. The young boy awoke just before dawn and gently shook his father's shoulder, 'Dad, wake up. It's time to get up.' His father mumbled, 'Give me a while longer. I'll be up soon.' The boy waited for half an hour before trying again to wake his father, repeatedly shaking his shoulder and saying, 'Dad, it is time to get up.'

Realizing that his father was going to have difficulty arising, the boy knew that time was wasting. He called Doodly to follow him, and they went off to look under rocks and fallen branches to find worms so as to have bait to catch fish.

Soon enough he had collected five worms and called the dog to come fish with him at the side of the river. Two hours later, he had caught three big ones. As he pulled each one to the shoreline, he called to Doodly to come have a look. The dog rushed over excitedly, grabbing the fish and dragging it to dry land. The boy jumped up and down, saying, 'Go, Doodly!' each time placing the large fish into a bucket with river water to keep them fresh before scaling and gutting them.

When all this was done, the boy, with a purposeful spring in his step, went out to gather firewood so as to slow cook the rice before preparing the catch. While this was occurring, he climbed the nearest tree to gather some coconuts to have something to drink and some fat to mix in with the meal.

Finally, his father awoke. It was then one-o'clock. As he staggered out of the hut all groggy, he looked very surprised and said to his son, 'You've been fishing. You've got coconut, and you've cooked the rice in preparation for the meal.'

Tenderly grasping his son's shoulder, with soft tears running down his face, he said, 'What a pleasant surprise. You are such a good boy! What an example you are. I am so happy. Come, sit by my side. I need to tell you something.' The boy sat down near his father and said, 'Yes, Dad, what do you need to tell me?'

'About five years ago, I was bitten by a mosquito and, as a consequence, caught African sleeping sickness. I have a difficult time waking up, and this has prevented me from living my life all these years in a way that I'm proud of. This is why I came to see you, because I had lost so much in these last five years. This made me realize my behavior of absence towards you needed to be fixed.

Now, I have discovered my son, and you have found your father. I am so proud of you. You are so not what I expected, and you could have misunderstood my sleeping illness, seeing it as a negative, but you didn't.'

With tears of gratitude rolling down his cheeks, he hugged his son. 'Let's eat and enjoy the food you have prepared and spend the rest of the afternoon playing catch with Doodly and exploring the nearby rainforest together.'

The next few days passed harmoniously as the boy and the father discovered one another. They were both blessed.

My dear disciples and visitors to the mango grove, look back upon your childhood, and keenly observe who you are right now. I am asking you to see which recovery, which story belongs to you: the first, which is a *curse* or the second that is a *blessing*? How have you arranged your memories as a child and how has this affected you as an adult?

Can you not see that the first memory of discordance belonged to the youngster's own construction of that past circumstance and was totally based on his emotional bias?

How has this affected you in your present moment? Are you looking back at your childhood right now?

Can you see that there are definitely two possibilities that belong to the first scenario? If you have a memory of your childhood characterized by negativity, when you go to locate and examine your past as the truth of your present moment, are you not doing harm to yourself and to your parent that you are assigning blame to?

Or can you concede, and realize, you could have been different right now if you saw your past as missed opportunities, thus transforming your bad memory into who you could have possibly been? I know this subject is very complex in the beginning, but this is the *Passerby* principle applied to your recall.

This concept has many layers within it. I am touching upon these intricate details to allow you to obtain a clear reference so that you may understand the disharmonious timeline compared with the harmonious sequences within the events you have just witnessed.

We will expand upon this subject within its entirety soon enough, using the tale of the boy and the father as a catalyst. This further establishes a deeper understanding of the principle of *Not Doing* oneself in comparison to completely *Doing* everything without question. Recapitulation must be examined."

"Master, can you speak more about that and how this process is so misunderstood within the variables of one's memory?"

"The reason why I asked you to look at the attitude that is vindictive, disappointed, and sour within the boy's approach towards his father, is to show how memory can be seen very clearly from two perspectives. Firstly, discontentment reaches for many variables in order to apply the manipulative aspects of one's personality upon another, to derive an outcome that benefits the manipulator.

If you look back in your own history and be totally honest, when you consider your past or your present moments, can you find any feeling within that reveals to you your own need to shame and then blame—and, by applying this twinned burden, obtain leverage of guilt through these devious means?

If this has happened to anyone here, know this: That is not your original nature. There is no need for me to say any more. You don't need to go back to your past to find out who you are right now, do you?

If you do recognize this behavior, have you not leveraged your influence to justify keeping somebody that may be innocent of your accusations, whether it be a parent or a friend, in a position that suits you?

Have you not captured the person that you are remembering within the prison of your own mind? Whenever you get the chance, will you not remind them of this? Are you not their prison guard at this particular point? It is such a neat little trap, this weaponized form of remembrance.

Though another person may have missed their opportunity to meet you in a time and space that has passed, to imprint dysfunctional perceptions within your present moment is a passive-aggressive stance wholly brought about through your insistence upon your own righteous bias. Entrapping the object of one's focus in this way is not only untenable but reveals an enormous poverty within.

This is the first complex scenario. The second is something people do not come upon very often, for it is extremely rare.

The original purity of the person in the first scenario learned to apply their *Doings* within their own flawed reflection. In the second one, they simply remained fluidly innocent, absorbing the frequencies of what had occurred and transforming them into a feeling of generosity.

There is no shame, nor blame applied to bring a person upon their guilt in the second scenario. What I am leading you to here is very simple and truly obvious—but this will not be easily seen if there is one ounce of resentment within a person's perception.

Carefully consider what I am saying. *Be open and aware; be your truly beautiful self.* Does this give you a feeling of vulnerability? Definitely! Does it open you to the world in a way which makes you sensitive toward everything coming at you? Absolutely! All I am suggesting here is that you make a choice to find your internal stability, not to react, but to be who you are really meant to be.

There are two poisons in the world to be mindful of—both the sender and the receiver from the negative scenario. This dysfunctional responsivity is a curse. Like Shiva's drum, the feedback loop between two resonant fields is generative, and can either be destructive or beneficial. Now, can you see that there are also two antidotes within the sender and the receiver? This is the blessing.

It is simple. *Be your open, loving, beautiful self* so that your voice may ascend in the moment for you to truly be you. This is sweet, something that you can digest and transform into the nourishment of your own reflective wisdom. It is your choice to be made.

So, take the world upon your chest. Struggle with it in the right way. Don't battle with it the wrong way. Also, don't be right or wrong. Be neutral and discover what arises from this. There is the true path.

The discernment of missed opportunities works like this—and here is where forgiveness of oneself and someone else appears. Ask yourself, whichever scenario is within you: *Did that person miss their opportunity to meet me? Did I miss my opportunity to meet them? Have I missed the opportunity to be myself? And: Did they not also miss their opportunity to be who they're really meant to be?*

This is where true compassion arises, not only for someone else but for yourself. Have we all not made mistakes in life? Once we've realized this, don't we automatically adjust the direction of our path to accommodate what was overlooked?

When this occurs, we can only love where love was absent. If this profound feeling is not there, understanding replaces it. But doesn't that comprehension then reach its hand of communion to the next *Being* you meet?

You must realize that love and understanding were our original *Doings*. Isn't it strange that now they have been inverted to become our *Not Doings*, which create abundance and joy and happiness that arise from within? Here is your next profound situational attunement to come to terms with. In the first scenario, love was hidden. In the second scenario, love is hidden. But in the initial one, it was not felt, while in the second, it is overwhelmingly evident."

THE UNDOING

"Master, I have a dear friend that I am deeply concerned about as they are on the edge of life and very near to their end. When I go to visit, I become aware of how I am drawn into their desperation. I have been your loving student for many years and don't know how to cope with this situation. Can you please advise me? What should I do?"

The Mango Grove Master, listening attentively, said to his disciple, "I cannot instruct you on how to enter the household of your friend with information that will pertain to yourself and them simultaneously.

I know that you ask me from the depth of your heart

what to do. I can only say, in true honesty, that in this situation it is very important to understand that every moment that you abide within has the secrets of life and death encoded within it. But can you obtain this wisdom? That is the question.

To plan to be somewhere before you are there is a mistake. From my heart, I cannot advise you what to *do*, but I can reveal what *not to do*.

Go to your friend without motive. Leave your heart open wide. Be an absolute representative of their feelings on the point that your internal subtleties begin to decode them. Yet, understand that not every micro-gesture can be spoken to.

At the end of one's life, a person's perception is already starting to open up and because of this, they will notice you realizing them. This, in turn, will create a sense of comfort for the dilemma they are facing.

You must open your heart to such a degree that the true influx of what is meant to be communicated on a very deep level will give you the capacity to recognize—via those subtle impulses of discernment—your own sense of free will. This quality of *Being* will identify multiple timeline convergences within the linear process for we are all subject to the variables that reveal themselves within the socially deterministic framework.

In other words, attune your awareness by utilizing all the areas of multiplicity in the same way we hear an echo returning to us from the abyss. This is the drum skin, which is all the compartmentalized acoustic phenomena revealing the dance of life.

What I am saying is that life is complex, and only you can see which stepping-stone to stand on as you rush across the river, reflexively landing upon the only one that is available to reach the other shore and hoping that you do not slip and fall.

We are all faced with this process. And no matter what we do or how devoted we are, our destiny will reveal itself to us as the event of falling headfirst into the waters of life and getting soaking wet. This is a form of determinism that is always attempting to drown free will. There is only one way to deal with this: Be seriously happy at all times.

Let's now return to the dilemma of your friend. Realize, they are coming upon themselves in a way they have not experienced before and are now facing the inevitable truth of what they are confronted with.

Your tenderness and sorrow for their circumstances must be spontaneous and only reveal the kindness of your heart speaking to their needs so as to bring them comfort. In other words, you meet them on their journey, not traveling upon the assumptive motive that wishes to intervene through my words that you want to communicate to them as comfort because you feel inadequate.

Go to the situation unclad. Be naked within your perception. Allow yourself to be dressed in the garments which will be given to you by your friend. Then you will know what to say. *Being, Knowing, and Not Doing* must be applied to this circumstance so as to arrive upon the perception that is awaiting you.

To accompany somebody at the end of their journey is a monumental task. I, too, have encountered this within my life. Realize, these are very subtle qualities that you will learn to harmonize. *Our simple, beautiful self is all we can be* when faced with the inevitability of the *Unknown.*

We all will be confronted with this in one way or another. The teachings that I have been disseminating throughout the years have contained within them the secret of living and dying simultaneously—the art of *Being, Knowing, and Not Doing* another person. The art of *Not Doing* oneself.

Practicing these techniques, you will discover that you can sit within one hundred percent of your own internal quietude and realize what is to be done next. I have advised you many times over the years to take the frequency that sits inside of your chest and deliver it to the ones that are dear to you as love and devotion. This will allow you to transmute any dissonant acoustics that have been passed to you from someone whose input was harmful.

When you transcend that discord and embody a feeling

of tenderness towards the ones you love, what will be stripped from you are not only the bad feelings received but the shape of the clothing that wishes to dress you in the mood of their *ghost*.

The moment you grasp the hand of your beloved and kiss them on the cheek, your gesture has deep implications. Your sincere embrace will relay the substance of your internal fortitude to stand true in your act of devotion.

Once your companion sees you're open to them within your own nakedness, they realize irrefutably that *you are one hundred percent your beautiful, loving self* that receives only them through this act of *divine communion.*

Remember, we are a mirror that does not look into its own reflection yet substantiates feeling through each *Being's* internal process. Once this sacred geometry establishes its rightful place, the act of *Being* yourself becomes the divinity within.

Here is where you travel upon the discipline of disciplines, for how can we possibly say that this inner beauty does not exist, when only the heavenly communion of your kindness is presented. To be a genuine conduit—to your husband or your wife, your brothers or sisters—is to fully be on the path that presents itself to you.

Once you realize that the correct garment covers your nakedness, only then can you step forward to express the inexpressible. When neither *thief* nor *ghost* exists, the *divine* appears. There are many things to learn that cannot be intellectually understood. The delicate equilibrium that is one's life path is all that matters."

"Master, can you please explain why you are teaching us like this?"

"It is very studious of you to realize there is a point of graduation within these techniques. Holding someone's hand and kissing them on the cheek evolves into a very subtle micro-gesture. This tenderness is one of the most direct ways to take a step toward the *divine*.

When you encounter a newborn child, isn't it natural to kiss them on the cheek while embracing their whole *Being* and simultaneously pulling them to your heart center?

Remember, I said we are like a mirror. We emulate the purity of that child by giving back its own innocence; but it is more than this—we reflect back the *divine* that reaches towards us. Then, don't we truly become its embodiment? Is this not what we, within our own evolutionary process, must eventually come upon?

When we practice the technique of *Being, Knowing, and Not Doing* somebody who has become lost, *Not Doing* them is the first step to arrive upon our ability not to judge. Thus, we dissolve our *Knowing* and enter into one of the first forms of forgiveness so that we can graduate this dissonant frequency as an act of devotion.

We indirectly love that person, thereby releasing ourselves and them simultaneously. This is a soft collision, which is one of two possibilities. The other is the principle of the hard collision. Both affect our timelines.

Now we are beginning to enter more deeply into the principle of the *Passerby*. This is the undressing of one's self-reflection. In other words, this is the *Not Doing* of what we think we *Know*. And it is the only way to reverse-engineer the expectations embedded within motive.

BE IN THE WORLD BUT NOT OF IT

In the temple of my Master, I was introduced to various ancient texts. At no point was I asked to read these doctrines. I was instructed by my teacher to lay down and listen and allow myself to drift in and out of consciousness while they were being read aloud.

The old Tibetan knew that I would be faced with many different obstacles, so he recited the Upanishads and all the sacred Vedas, and other secret texts that are so holy they cannot be understood by the interpretive system of the waking mind. They must be hidden deep within one's consciousness so as to arrive upon their elusiveness through the mundane world calling them to the surface.

I would like to speak with you now about the ancient *Book of the Dead*, but not in a way that you would expect.

This sacred knowledge was put together by some very special, talented individuals who translated their experience, as Tibetans, about this elusive subject. To understand this text with crystal clear discernment, you must look at their writings from the reality of their own bias.

Even though these monks were absolutely right in terms of what they had written, the secret key to this knowledge is to understand the very essence of the principle of the *Passerby*. What clothing are you dressed in, right now?"

The Grove Master looked up as he asked this, gently acknowledging all the visitors under the Bodhi tree, including his disciples.

"I see many nationalities here before me. Not only have you come from the nearby communities, there are also some who have travelled from other continents that are far from our shores.

You are wearing different garments. Your hair is cut in a way that is culturally acceptable, and you have different languages; yet you come here, and all speak English. Nevertheless, when you ask me questions, I hear your accent. The skin of your drum beats a different rhythm in comparison to another. The frequency of this emanation, which permeates the grove while you communicate, gives rise to subtle nuances of your person.

I would ask you all to now realize that the *Book of the Dead* was conceived of by Tibetans. Will not their dreams be dressed in a monk's attire? Will not what confronts them reach into their consciousness whilst they slumber, as the memory of their waking world?

Will they not see the demons and deities of their culture? And when they brought this sacred scripture to the world, would they not have been faced with the bias of other nationalities, asking: *How can we apply such specificity to our death? Are we to believe that what confronts you will confront us?*

The secret of this sacred book is simple to translate. What you have dreamed of in your waking world, what you *Do* that cannot be undone, will follow you in your slumber. Is this not the truth? I sit here in India and speak to you. Will you tonight dream about Shiva because of me? Will you conceive of the deities within the *Tibetan Book of the Dead*?

You will only dream your daytime reality, in comparison to all you've been taught since you've been born.

When I look upon the people assembled in front of me and you ask me a question, will I not then be contained within its full implications? And am I not your answer, reflected upon your world through the purity of my response, which will have within it no identifiable points that depict my experience of life in comparison to your inquiry, and will inevitably lead you back to yourself?

Sitting next to you is a person from a different country. They will experience an exact duplicate of themselves in comparison to my words related to you, yet their responsiveness bounces from their own bias, which is the drum being beaten from their cultural perspective.

This is the reason why I have taught you *Being, Knowing, and Not Doing*—so that *Not Doing* will beat upon the subtleties of your *Doings* to be undone. To understand this is to recalibrate what you think you know so you may encounter the unthinkable notion of knowing something that is not thought. When this occurs, you graduate from your own bias to utterly come upon the unexpected within yourself.

This is the face of *No Place* within your humanness. Once you learn to apply this transformational technique, you begin to reverse-engineer anything and everything that has been constructed around you, as you journey back to your origin of emptiness.

Now that you realize there is a skin on the drum that beats upon the general understanding of your interpretive *Knowing*, this bias also must be let go of. Once you comprehend this, graduation begins to occur. But remember, this cannot be intellectually pursued.

Within the full implications of releasing yourself from your bias, your intellect will cease to exist. Here is where that modus operandi will become neutralized. Once emptiness is integrated, instead of seeking, you will be sought out. And now I will show you how I came upon this wisdom."

The Old Sage looked at his disciples, "I am very long-winded today, but nothing like the donkey," he laughed, bouncing up and down like jelly.

"The reason why I am speaking like this to you all is to allow you to see that death is very transparent. It will give back to you the same food you have eaten. It will see you in the clothing you are dressed within when you enter.

In Christian theology, when a person reaches the thresholds of *Heaven*, this has been described as *the pearly gates*, for the pearl reflects back to the person who they are.

As we enter this etheric portal, we take with us everything that we were. This in essence is the code that will pre-program the *Unknown* to reveal the self that the individual has brought with them, in all its diversity.

Carried within this signature are joys and sorrows, along with all of the self-perceived transgressions of one's character. What we will then be faced with is all that is not noble so as to test our ability to pass.

We will remember all the feelings contained within our lifetime, which will manifest upon a transparent screen that reflects back the imagery that may bring upon us who we were. And this will be more than confronting, for our perception will be nine times clearer than it was when we were living.

We will be faced with everything that we neatly hid behind our own drawn curtain of denial within the consciousness of the life that we have just left.

This reveals what can be transported into the transition between life and death. And what I am going to describe now are particular moods such as pride, greed, lust, envy, gluttony, wrath and sloth, which are transferred by one's resistances into the Bardo.

Does this not sound similar to the demons that can be found within the descriptions of the *Tibetan Book of the Dead*? The only difference is how they figuratively form, in comparison to the consciousness of the dying person.

But you must remember: These demons are only there because the deities are dressed within the awareness of the person being confronted. If you can face them at this point by having no fear, they will be transformed, like a *Not Doing* of your *Doings*, into a welcoming embrace.

If this cannot be achieved, the fear that will consume your soul will cause you to turn and run, to find something softer that feels safe and comforting. This truly is the most elaborate trap of one's humanness for that seeking will send you back into a rebirth because of what you could not face within the transition.

What threatens you is safe, and what is safe is truly threatening. Here you will be sent back through opening the door of comfort that is your decision to flee what you are meant to confront. For those of you who have ears to hear and eyes to see, recognize this warning.

Being returned to where you came from will be utterly consuming via the fact that each door that you can escape through has an implication. Is this not what happens in life? Bardo is nothing but a mirror. Yet remember, the face of your own transgressions will dress their masks in a horror that you have obtained within the life you've lived.

But do not despair. If you practice diligently *Being, Knowing, and Not Doing*—and all the principles contained therewithin—it will not be as hard as you imagine. Bardo is the most dangerous transition only because of our inability to realize what we are meant to apply within life. Here is where our *Not Doings* must become operational. I hope you can now see this is where the true burdens within liberty are hidden."

"Master, so many times during these transmissions, I have been moved to tears by your words. How can I know if I'm simply engaging in my emotional predispositions, which are coloring newly-found understanding, or experiencing true feeling arising from realizations?

And furthermore, as we walk upon our timelines, interacting with the world and those around us, how do we know the difference between self-pity that services emotional disruption and true feeling that can lead us deeper into our understanding of *As others are, so am I?"*

"Allow yourself to have your upheavals. Let your burdens arise to be seen. They are a cleansing. But, if when your tears form you notice your emotions seeking recognition, you will then comprehend the difference between the two.

Let your simple self step forward to be in a loving embrace towards the world, not drawing on any part of your tears to engage. Here is where you will come upon your sacredness. It will undo your motives, simultaneously revealing your tenderness. The question that you've asked, you can answer.

Are your footsteps not impressions left within your journey? Allow the heavenly waters of your shorelines to wash them from your view. Never once have we asked the sea to remove our imprinted steps, yet it is done. This is all that needs to be pondered. Are you not the waters that will encompass your shorelines?"

"Master Turya, you told us about your childhood at the

temple and the Tibetan monks' immense patience combined with such purity, where no blame, no shame, and no guilt are contained within the whole surroundings. I am really fascinated by such a state of *Being*. Can you please tell me, does this relate to the idea of repentance being practiced generally in most religious traditions and in our village? Since this often associates with a sort of guilt stemming from the past and being brought to the present, what is the true meaning of repentance? Is that also a *Knowing* or a bias?"

"To answer your question from a Christian theological perspective, generally speaking, repentance refers to a state of guilt. I believe under no circumstances should our transgressions be given to a priest to be cleansed, unless that person has purified themselves of this very bias.

Are you not the priest and the confessor simultaneously? We all must attend to our own work and never expect anyone else to do it for us. In other words, when you begin to realize how to proceed, you will know that a middleman is never meant to be between you and your destiny."

THE PASSERBY

I will now demonstrate for you how the mysteriousness of the *Unknown* revealed to me my own graduation through its emptiness acknowledging my non-responsiveness to the *thieves* and *ghosts* that populate the dream state that is the first doorway one enters upon their death.

I have advised you all along, *Not to Do* other people and, simultaneously, *Not to Do* yourself. Many years ago, when you were very young in your apprenticeship, I prescribed to you a technique that I would like to remind you of now.

When you go to bed at night, watch yourself transitioning from waking to sleeping. As this occurs, do you hear your own voice speaking to you? What is this phenomenon helping you manifest?

The auditory presence reveals your internal reality that is coming upon you. Or you may just appear within that scene, seemingly unconscious of the *Doings* that are unfolding.

How does the dream allow you to understand what you may be confronted with when dying? See this very simply. This is the truest challenge that you must comprehend. And when you reflect upon this imagery that is being discussed right now, isn't this the very complexity that reveals your burden that must be undone?" the Mango Grove Master asked in a cautionary tone.

"Do not the voices that manifest in the dreaming images also show you your cultural predispositions? Isn't that exactly the same as the world *Does* you and you *Do* the world?

When I say culture, I mean more than the country you are born in. The emotions and desires that you secretly harbor will reveal the island that you have become. Realize, these are your self-reflective biases.

The secret behind watching yourself go to sleep is to allow the dream to *Do* itself, but what's important is for you *Not to Do* the dream. This is one of the great mysteries of our transition from life to death and then into a new incarnation. Remember, what I am describing for you now is only a rudimentary phase, via the fact that you are still contained within a visionary construct composed of your emotions.

I want to show you how to go beyond this so that you don't have to return but may advance upon your path of awakening, wherever that will lead you, and not be led into alternate options that become devastating because of the choices you have made, as a result of your enflamed emotional responsivity.

As your teacher, I must search for my own thresholds. Who is there to instruct me while I'm guiding you? And how do I know this wisdom is real? Remember, I am not inquiring for myself. I am asking you to consider that what I am about to say will not come upon you until you learn to stop the world the same way that I have—by simply *Not Doing* it.

This is the secret of secrets.

Consider this carefully. You must be aware of your *thief* and your *ghost*. They will attempt to replicate my words into their justifiable points to maintain dominion. They will sit far away from a mountain and paint a picture, or for many years provide fruit that looks sweet yet is sour.

Beware of what I have instructed you to witness and honestly watch yourself so as not to betray your own journey. I know you grasp what I am saying, but this is not meant to be merely spoken of. It is to be applied through your own *Not Doings*."

The visitors of the grove listened in a deep introspective silence to everything the Mango Grove Master was saying.

"Let me show you how the threshold of graduation came upon me many years ago and simply whispered: *You are ready*—even though I never considered myself prepared in any way. Am I not *Not Doing* something right now?

I have been tested by the emptiness. You will see through my story how I became qualified to accompany somebody on their journey in the transition from this life to the next. This experience has to do with me being dreamt by the *Unknown* so as to gauge my reactivity to the vision being enacted before me.

Within the imagery presented, I found myself knocking at my friend's door. As I entered, I noticed that he did not see me. From my right, a woman passed in front of me. I saw that she was naked and seeking the attention of my friend while slightly acknowledging me. She walked back to where she came from. I must now clarify one important detail. This woman appeared to be my wife, whom I love dearly. Can you imagine how this would trigger a response? But I was stable and unaffected. I knew this reality was not real.

I then approached her and said, 'I can see your desire to be noticed. Why does he ignore you? And why do you pretend you can't be seen by me?'

Standing up, the woman aggressively grabbed my shoulders, pushed me to the front door and forcefully ushered me down the path and away from the house, where she began loudly shouting insults. Attempting to trigger a mood of shame and despair within me, she was saying, 'Everything that you have taught in your life is ridiculous. You are a failure.' I stopped very gently and listened carefully to what was being said.

In my heart, I did not forget that my wife would not, under any circumstances, speak to me like this. She is a beautiful, soft person of much integrity. I have never heard her speak in a harsh way towards any person, and I knew without a doubt that this was an illusion attempting to unseat my clarity.

All my years of *Not Doing* the waking world revealed at that point that the dream could not *Do* me. Noticing everything I was witnessing; I did not react. I was free and walked beyond the scene into a white light that suddenly appeared.

Here I must mention that there are many different colors that will tempt your attention to want to be absorbed within their luminosity. This is what happened with me. I have experienced more than one type of white light. I recognized what this one was, and I knew on a very deep, visceral level that it was safe to enter it.

Your destiny will engulf you, and if you are clear it will be obvious how to proceed. I cannot advise anything beyond this, because there is no way to pre-empt what will occur—this would be folly on my part. Unfortunately, you really can't help anyone once they have entered. The work has to be done *before* you die.

When I reached this threshold in my own journey, I found myself within an eternal emptiness that did not call upon itself to be witnessed. As I looked into it, there was no echo of me to be found.

It was then that I was confronted with the implications of the vastness before me. As I looked into this endlessness, I became aware of a transparent film, far in the distance of eternity, pressing towards me. Deep within that, I suddenly saw the contours of a face emerging.

I will not describe to you how it looked because it was exclusively for me to witness, but this face of the *Unknown* was the skin of the largest drum that I have ever seen. To enter its emptiness with impunity one must not bring any part of themselves that will disrupt their experience. To pass through this membrane is to leave my worldly confines. No part of me from the past may follow.

If even a fraction of a grain of sand remains, this membrane will bounce me back to the world of suffering that I have diligently practiced to leave. And upon re-entry, there is no certainty that the family that I will be reborn into will have any idea about how to retrieve what I have so conscientiously and faithfully remembered up to this moment.

I came upon the realization that creation was instructing the small pinpoint of my awareness to become absent of itself so as to learn the lessons I needed to graduate towards—and this is the most difficult subject to attempt to explain.

Realize, you cannot expect the entrance from life to death to be anything other than you. The question is: Who is behind the imagery of the story of my life that I have just conveyed through this dream? Even I can't fathom this.

The doorway of my future, which is my destiny, is revealed. Who is my Master and how did he learn to teach me in such a way? I feel humbled to accept that this cannot be understood.

My dear disciples, the white light is your enlightenment. If another color appears, this could possibly be a doorway towards your rebirth. This eventuality is totally contingent on how much fear has manifested.

There is *Human Being, Knowing, and Doing* within its continuous repetition. And then we have *Human Being, Knowing, and Not Doing* our reality, which is the first step towards reverse-engineering our outwardly bound consciousness so as to return it to its source.

To repeat once again: *Knowing and Doing* essentially must translate the *Doing* of certainty into an area of *Not Doing*, which brings that frequency into its appropriate position of *Inaction*. When this occurs, the disciple must take the sound of their own drum and transform its rhythm into service and love.

Once this happens, an inaudible frequency arises. It cannot be seen, heard, or felt—yet, when realized, it is actually *seen, heard, and felt*. This can only be described as a revelation of the *divine*. The eternal rhythm manifests from the source of *No Place* that appears within human attention. Here is where the mask of one's identity disappears from view.

Our gestures then become connected to the fabric of reality in such a way that we have thus reverse-engineered our reflective consciousness to become aware of a new phenomenon. That drum's skin is so thin that if one is careful, we may disappear from ourselves into an area of awareness so far removed from *Knowings and Doings* that even our *Not Doings* look like *Doings*.

The only way, my dear disciples, to cope with what I have just transmitted is to *be your most beautiful, innocent, loving self*, presenting who you truly are on the level of your heart. Know that from behind your eyes, contained within your listening power, your arising wisdom will allow you to be strong and kind simultaneously.

Yet, remember: If at any point you fall into the trap which is presented through the content of that dream, you will plunge headlong into its nightmare, thus being chased to the four corners of your reality, bouncing upon the delicate drum. That echo chamber will surround and transport you back to the center of your narrative, which will then determine your return through searching for the most comfortable corner that you believe will give you some sense of relief.

In many ways, our planet *Earth* imprisons us. Not because it is malevolent. Only because we enter our own strange rooms and lock the door behind us, ricocheting around the walls in a mansion that has tens of thousands of chambers for us to abide within.

We proclaim that we don't know how to leave, and in that moment of proclamation the key to escaping these realities suddenly disappears from our view. Thus we forget, hiding ourselves from our *divine discernment* with the power of an indestructible bias.

I hope that by now it is obvious that you have to wait for

the frequency of graduation to come upon you. And you will never know what it contains and how it will arrive. This is the rule. Does anybody have any questions?"

One of the disciples asked, "Master, can you please explain what *your simple, beautiful self* is?"

"We are all born with a fundamental nature that has its own exclusive expression. Though we are similar, we differ in many ways. When we come upon the simplicity of ourselves, we discover unity, happiness, kindness, and understanding. The fundamental rules of nature appear in front of us and require us to decode, through the sincerity of our love and devotion, what is meant to be realized.

This can only be attained through subduing one's personal motive, thereby adjusting to the world at large in a way that harmonizes us. We dress ourselves with this sound-wave that then becomes sacred geometry that will avail itself when we gain access to the wisdom contained within *Being our simple, loving selves.* For you to fathom this, you must enter Bardo before your death. Only then will you realize what is required of you.

HEAVEN AND EARTH

"Remember, years ago, I spoke to you about *siddhis*. This is a form of consciousness that comes upon an individual through their persistent devotion toward the *divine*. Nadis are like the stars in the sky but instead of looking up, we gaze within to discover their shining light. They echo in our *Being*, revealing where we are. It is how we respond to them that determines what we will become.

Throughout my life, I have been blessed with many *siddhis*, all corresponding to the centralized power of my heart. Their natural manifestation is an epiphany that sustains itself upon one's internal revelations toward the contours of that power. They are like an individual that we meet who causes us to notice something special is occurring.

But the secret within the *nadi's* representation is to know when to let go of its influence so as to not be breached via the content of one's recognition in such a way that it would become corrupted. To be sustained within that momentary insight without possessing it is to release oneself from it so that realizations may reformulate within the heart of the one who has had the fortune to notice that *nadi*. How this is applied to your life is a subtle mystery that can be decoded."

"Master, can you show us an example of a *siddhi* from your own experience that will relay to us how the principle is applied so we can attempt to understand your philosophy?"

"Firstly, let's look at the people we meet who are the ones that awaken within us our dormant memories. They are who we are meant to collide with, but in the beginning that may not be obvious. This is the reason why we use *Being, Knowing, and Not Doing*, to identify the arising frequency that is not apparent until the *Doing* is undone via one's *Inaction*.

This is where the hidden sound wave manifests to be observed. At this stage, however, we must patiently wait for this acoustic phenomenon to gently come upon us as a feeling from within.

Though this frequency may initially seem to be kind of skittish, this is not completely accurate. However, if the inaudible process of ascension is in any way whatsoever disturbed through the assumption that one is entitled to *Know*, the *Not Doing* will immediately collapse from one's view.

This is what we are dealing with and why it is necessary to modify one's outwardly-bound communication toward an inward exploration of *Inaction*. This may sound complex, but we have to be faced with these forms of diversity in order to evolve beyond the barriers of our resistance.

Not Doing is expressed as gestures that redefine one's internal contours, thus reorganizing this perceived phenomenon to be re-revealed to one's consciousness. Emergence is a subtle frequency that arises from *Not Doing* one's *Doings*.

Even though transformation denotes another kind of *Doing*, here it is a manifestation of non-action, or reverse-engineered perception, that will give way to a feeling within the chest as an angelic joy arising. This, in essence, reveals one of the sources of our animation.

Remember, I have previously described this heavenly braille to you as a form of dexterity that becomes inwardly aware of itself through the containment field of the human form and ultimately lights the eternal fire of the heart center.

Is not ascension a vacuous manifestation of form itself?

We will come back to these principles later. For now, let's focus on *Heaven and Earth*.

We have two qualities within our humanness. One is *earthly bound*; the other is directed towards our *heavenly process*. What I am about to explain must be integrated so as to comprehend the full implications of my philosophy.

Before we return to our discourse about *Knowing and Doing*, and thus *Not Doing* those *Knowings*, there is something happening within my teachings that you haven't noticed.

When I asked you, as young boys, to stand by the saplings within the mango grove, directing your attention to notice the subtle feelings arising within you, I was very gently instructing your body how to become aware of five preliminary mechanisms within your *Being*.

When these elements become harmonized, the process of one's individual power will begin to arise as *siddhis*—dormant manifestations that relate to one's internal *nadis* becoming active. This is done through observing the physical processes of the body being awakened to the realization that it is right in the middle of *Heaven and Earth*.

The planet beneath our feet represents magnetism. *Heaven* above us is experienced as electric vacuousness. These are the first two elements.

When you stood still next to our young saplings many years ago, my instruction was to allow you to become aware of the mycelia complex within the root system of the old grove reaching towards them as a form of communion. The old trees will connect by attending to the young roots and calling upon them to realize that their awakening is contingent upon the process of that vital exchange. Is this not similar to what has happened between all of you and myself?

This fabric is everywhere; it is the most subtle, interweaving quality of our universe. It is a fundamental law. To fathom this is all that matters, and it is what the general populace of our planet has forgotten to recognize within its entirety. Realize this: The ground is below us, the sky is above. We are in the center."

Picking up a beautiful round rock, he continued. "Imagine now that this pebble is our human condition." Looking toward the pond near the Bodhi tree, Master Turya's eyes were smiling as he said, "Watch very carefully," and, with a sudden flick of his wrist, he flung it into the still waters.

"When it hits the surface and begins to sink to the bottom, can you notice that the space the pebble first occupied is now an indentation within the waters which causes a bubble to appear? This is our vacuous nature, the rising force, a heavenly process.

As the pebble descends, the moment that the bubble releases from its form is where we are truly suspended within our human condition. As the rock slowly sinks to the depths and the bubble escapes to the surface, this is where we are mysteriously animated.

The bubble is *Heaven*; where the pebble sinks is *Earth*, and slightly in between these two phenomena is where we reside as human beings.

We have now three major elements: *Heaven, Man,* and *Earth*. There are two more factors to explain within this trinity that will cause us to evolve, and this is one of the primary mechanisms that we need to comprehend: how a *siddhi* or a power arises within.

Remember, it cannot be seen, felt, or heard. Yet, when it comes upon you, you will feel, see, and hear the echoes of its eternal reflection arriving upon itself within one's human form to assist in the unfolding of your evolution.

Now, I wish to explain the fundamental foundation of

how to come upon oneself through the rising and descending process within our *Being,* known as the communion of *Heaven and Earth within Man.* How we discover this within ourselves is usually by being taught to recognize it.

The next two qualities that combine with the trinity of *Heaven, Man, and Earth* are hidden within the rising and descending force—and this can initially be seen through activating these principles via physical movement.

In the beginning of your apprenticeship when I asked you to stand by the saplings in the mango grove, I directed you to extend the very rear of your skull towards the sky so as to open the vertebrae in your neck. This is known as the *heavenly gate.*

While standing, simultaneously gently lift your hips, with your knees slightly bent so as to open the vertebrae that extend downwardly from your kidneys to your coccyx. This opens the *earthly gate,* ultimately activating these two principles within the bioenergetics of our human form, which you will realize is mobilizing our electro-magnetic predisposition to become an antenna.

The next technique to focus upon is to ascend and descend within your body via the rivers of your mind. As you sink through your physical form whilst standing, a feeling will gently cascade downwards inside your physicality until it arrives at the bottom of your feet.

At this point, two small pillars of light enter the ground. Rising from the feet, back up through the body, you ascend until you reach the top of your head. Your antenna will then appear, connecting you with *Heaven*. Both of these connections of *Heaven and Earth*, below the feet and above the head, must at no time be withdrawn so as to create the alchemical process of these two qualities mixing within the center of *Man*.

We are still only exploring three elements so far: *Heaven, Earth, and Man*. What is necessary to comprehend beyond this point is the ascension process, which relates to the *earthly aspect of Heaven* and the *heavenly aspect of Earth*.

When one sinks to the ground, this gesture pulls electric vacuousness down to the magnetic field of the *Earth*. When one's body arises, this draws the magnetic field of the *Earth* upwards towards the electric vacuousness of *Heaven*.

To reiterate, we have an *earthly aspect of Heaven* descending, and a *heavenly process of Earth* arising. The electro-magnetic convergence of these two phenomena is ultimately alchemized within the very center of man. *As above, so below.*

Once *Heaven and Earth* are harmonized within you, through the complex evolutionary mechanisms of contact, you will realize the power inside of you.

Our task at this point is to decipher what appears within us that will become the path we walk upon as a sentient *Being*. This is absolutely contingent upon our own individual vibratory essence which, in the beginning, is governed by our physical configuration. In other words, the landscape of our *Beingness*: facial features, length of bones, internal predispositions, and so forth.

This is why it is imperative to understand *Being, Knowing, and Not Doing*, and what arises from realizing what is meant to be noticed. This will inevitably alert us to the principle of the *mustard seed*.

As it sits upon the *Earth*, half of it will enter the soil. The other portion will be above the surface. Here the philosophy of *as above, so below* manifests. Are not both halves contained within something? Are they not a reflection of each other within their different qualities?

When it finally roots towards the *Earth*, does it not simultaneously bud towards the *Heavens*? What appears at this point is a crack in its very center that reveals a disc of light expanding in all directions simultaneously. This, in essence, is the origin of our animation, where all possibilities appear.

We must delicately explore this, for many strange phenomena will rise to be noticed by the one who unlocks this secret.

And this is truly what Shiva meant in terms of the dance of life. Once you have obtained this equilibrium, the centralized plane awakens the delicate harmonization within our physical form in comparison to the animation of our source of light.

I will further explain this to you, my dear disciples, in the future. I will ask you to allow this to settle into your consciousness before we continue upon our journey."

"Oh, Master, are you asking us to wait again?" said one of the disciples playfully.

"Absolutely," the Master answered, smiling. Nevertheless, let me reiterate one more point in terms of the principle *as above, so below*.

Realize, whether it be *Heaven* or *Earth*, there will always be a harmonious confluence between the two. In other words, *Earth* has a little bit of *Heaven* within it, and *Heaven* cradles *Earth* within its reflection. Do you understand?" asked the Old Sage, searching the faces of the disciples for signs of confirmation before continuing.

"In summary, the *earthly process of Heaven* will mix with the *heavenly process of Earth*. In this way, nothing can be misunderstood. Harmonization reveals that imperfection is perfect, and, thus, perfection is imperfect. This balance will indicate the only place that is available for all *Beings* to stand in comparison to their evolutionary status.

If you have ears to hear, you will know that this is one of the secrets of the *Passerby*.

Now, let me convey to you another story so you can see how, once a *siddhi* has awoken to itself, it may allow you to travel upon your previous existences or timelines. The way this occurs is through minor glimpses. These are soft collisions that have major implications. It is like your past comes upon your present moment, knocking on the door of your internal hallways—and as you open to this experience, a certain amount of light will flood in and illuminate them.

I will show you how this strange event occurred for me, and you will realize through this explanation why I have said for so many years: *Don't be consumed with what presents itself to you because this may turn the power itself into a form of possession.*

Knowing this, let's get back to the story.

I awoke within a vision. This was the light that entered

my internal hallways. As I travelled upon it, it led me to a past timeline. I saw my devoted disciple standing over his transitioning Master. I was alive within my vision, yet I witnessed myself being guarded by my devotee in Tibet, during the moment of my death.

I could deeply feel his dedication and love for his Master as he stood so steadfastly by the side of my still body. Unbeknownst to him at that moment, I appeared as a subtle mist, which was in actuality his call to me to ask where I was. I believe it was his sincere feelings that pulled me to him so we could commune for a very tender moment of recognition.

This is when I felt him noticing me and, in an instant, I realized he saw me as a softly diffused light arising in front of him. His feelings of loss were suddenly nullified through this connection. He knew that I had landed safely within my new time continuum—my present lifetime—and was relieved that I had the power to return for that moment.

I know this is difficult to understand. I ventured back from around two hundred and eighty years in the future to the moment of my past death, into a timeline where we all know that this man, too, would have already passed on. To this day, it is hard for me to even fathom how this occurs. But in the same breath, within my heart, it is understood without any doubt.

This is not my first experience of re-engaging with that lifetime from my present continuum, and on the initial occasion, I was still living in both timelines concurrently.

All I can say is life is an unfolding mystery that will, at every point of awakening, tear down the walls of any bias so as to see that these doorways are continually open. This is one of the ways that the *nadis* within my present lifetime have opened up as a *siddhi*.

To reiterate, the power within the *nadi* that had appeared within my body in my present-day existence, allowed the veil of time to be opened for a split second, where my devotee and I both understood simultaneously what had taken place. Realize, the reason this occurred was only because of love and devotion, and that allowed me to say goodbye in a way which had immense value for both of us.

So, as I sit with you under the Bodhi tree at this moment, I recall love and devotion from two perspectives. Mine, as his teacher, and his, as the mastery to become all that he was meant to be within the power of that moment.

We shared that *siddhi* for an instant, even though the *nadi* within my living body awakened hundreds of years later, only to return with all that is of value: an unyielding devotion of the *Unknown* to speak through the simultaneous gain and loss—since within that loss there are so many things gained.

What becomes prominent as a result is not only the tenuous thread of devotion but also the ultimate realization that the *Unknown* travels upon everybody's lifetime like this. And this is difficult to comprehend. What presses upon our awareness, from a universal perspective, is nothing but devotion towards its progeny.

Are not all conscious *Beings* within our universes connected by this? That's why I have said to you, over and over again, *be your most beautiful, loving self,* for this is where you meet the *divine.*

Only from this standpoint can you accept your destiny in comparison to everything else that exists. For when we leave our physical existence, we are not only embraced by our own memories, we are engulfed within those eternal fluctuations. This is where we discover gratitude.

By realizing this, I now honor his memory in the same way he honors mine. Is this not love and devotion to the *Unknown*?

I would like to pay homage to my disciple through the recounting of this glimpse of my death in a previous incarnation. Am I not the departed Tibetan being tended to by his devotee? This riddle is all that matters. Love and devotion across lifetimes combine us into many points of unification. Maybe you will understand this in its entirety as the years pass you by, in correspondance with the potency of love and devotion that will develop within you.

You must realize that while I reveal my experiences to you, I am unlocking your own potential towards yourself. Each person has the most important power that can ever be arrived upon within them. It shines from within your chest like a drum that is beating upon your reality.

If it beats outwardly, it is still inextricably inwardly bound. If it beats inwardly, it is irreversibly externally bound. Not too dissimilar to a pebble being dropped in a pond, the ripples reach out to the furthest shores before softly returning to their source. Neither reality exists more prominently than the other.

One must learn to see that if a veil appears to be obscuring one's view, as you travel through this silk curtain, when you turn around to discover where it came from, it is going to become what it is.

The consciousness of man has many rooms that one can momentarily rest within. If you make the mistake to pause too long, cannot that chamber within that mansion suddenly possess you? I will now reveal a few of my experiences to demonstrate how I managed not to be trapped in any of these rooms."

The Old Sage, looking at one of his devotees, asked, "Do you remember inquiring, years ago, about something that occurred between myself and a visitor to the Mango Grove? Could you please recount this for all of us?"

"Yes, Master, I remember you were once demonstrating movements to us and a visitor entered the grove while you were teaching. He respectfully touched you on the shoulder so as to alert you that he had arrived.

Barely coming in contact with you, he bent forward as though a heavy weight was suddenly upon his shoulders. Then, immediately, his body jumped two feet back into the air, away from you, as if he were as light as a feather. I was shocked, as was he, but you continued teaching without even acknowledging that this had occurred. Why was that?"

"This is a simple thing to explain. It is a particular power that your body becomes aware of through diligently practicing the movements that I have shown you all these years.

At that stage of my life, I had strongly decided not to pursue this phenomenon which you witnessed. This power had been in my biofield since I was a teenager. There have been many instances where people even have had the sensations of the movements from my body grabbing their internal organs from at least fifteen to twenty feet away from where I stood. As you can imagine, this brought about many questions within them towards what I have achieved through all my practices.

From my early years, to the point you saw this happening with the man who sprang backwards upon touching me on the shoulder, I had resolved not to seek the development of these abilities. The question was within my heart: 'What else will come to me if I don't acknowledge this and let it pass me by?' I can say now, irrefutably, that when one door closes another will open.

And I do believe I made the right decision. But in saying this, it does not matter whether such abilities can be cultivated or not. If it happens by itself, without the intervention of intention, this is really the key to our growth as human beings in terms of *Not Doings* truly revealing themselves through the experience of one's *Inactions* coming to the surface to be seen.

I believe now that if I purposely pursue these abilities, at this stage of my life, I would not become lost in that pursuit. But if I would have followed that power in my youth, I doubt that I would be the man I am today. Can you see what was hidden and now what is revealed within my answer to your question?

It may appear that I have many powers beyond what seems to be your limited perception of what can be achieved. But the only worthwhile understanding that I have obtained in my life that nourishes me to my very bones is that love and kindness is all that matters. And in the same breath, as more *nadis* open up within my body, the more I obtain through what is being unveiled.

As you grow on your path as a human being, you will naturally feel excited to come upon what seems unobtainable. Yet as you travel towards your inevitable end, what will be revealed to you upon your last breath? Will it not be who you were and what you did with that? Here something deeply ethical will choose for us who we were. It is never contingent upon who we think we are.

Ponder this for one moment: Only within this reflection, will the whole of your life come upon you in one instant, whispering very gently to whom it is within you that manages who you are.

As I am expressing this statement towards you, my heart advances upon me, searching inwardly for you. And within this magnificent collision, we both disappear in that loving embrace.

THE POWER OF THE OLD TIBETAN

I would now like to reveal how the power of a *siddhi* came upon my Master in Tibet many years ago. Long before I tended this mango grove, when I was in my early teens, I observed the old Tibetan in a very strange situation with one of his disciples. Watching the whole sequence of events was extremely enlightening for me.

My Master was teaching an outsider who had come to visit the mountainous region where our temple was located. He had noticed that this young man was very powerful and invited him into the monastery for a few weeks to practice.

THE POWER OF THE OLD TIBETAN

At the very same time, the old Tibetan had begun to train one of his devotees to sit in stillness and observe what was occurring between himself and those he was teaching. He very delicately instructed him not to intervene in any way whatsoever, during or after the sessions.

This disciple's task was to pick up their guest from the village—to be polite and accommodating, yet not to speak of what was happening within the teachings that my Master was imparting.

As time progressed, I became aware of how this man who had been invited into the monastery began to open up about his life. He mentioned that there had been two specific individuals who had severely dominated him, attempting to crush the power that was naturally inherent within his *Being*.

The Old Tibetan could see that he needed to be released from his burden, which had colored his eyes in such a way that he would become reactive if he met another person who had power, just like my Master.

As I witnessed my teacher interacting with him, I

realized that his presence alone assured our guest that he could trust the Tibetan's guidance. In this circumstance he did not need to harbor any form of suspicion because of what he had experienced in his past.

My Master very carefully presented to him only who he was. Nothing more, nothing less. He knew it was unavoidable that the young man would recognize his immovable power and was guiding him to open up about the resistant echo that related back to his pain so that he could move forward unencumbered.

My Master proceeded within his teachings as carefully as possible so as not to trigger him in any way. He could see that he had much personal power but was being influenced by his past circumstances to such a degree that he was lost because of the resistant element that had taken root within him."

The Mango Grove Master mentioned to his disciples, "Watch very carefully what transpires between the Tibetan and this young man. His emotional bias is the cargo that those two individuals in his past, especially one of them, had intentionally transferred to his vessel. You will see how it is neatly hidden within his subtle predispositions, due to him not being totally aware of its influence, which was unrelentingly steering him away from his true path. Because of this, his power could not arise effectively. This is your first clue.

The reason why he was invited to the temple is that my master had noticed what was taking place within him and could see that his resources were being bypassed by his life path being directed toward the wrong destination as a result of his internal injuries.

Many people traveled to our village on a pilgrimage toward their enlightenment. The Old Tibetan would visit at certain times of the year so as to observe those that made this journey. This is when he noticed the young man's remarkable physical power and the potential of his internal light. Though he knew his experiences would be complex, he nevertheless invited him to the temple.

Now, a few days before our guest returned to his country of origin, the disciple began to question the young man as they made their way to the temple. 'What is it within you that the Master has brought to the surface for you to observe? How do you feel?'

Responding openly, he said, 'It has brought up an old feeling inside of me that I have battled with most of my life. In the past, one man had forced his will so strongly upon me that I did not want to live anymore. He was trying to make me stronger by attempting to destroy me. It is one of the tactics that they use in the armed forces.'

Upon hearing his answer, the disciple said, 'Oh!' in a tone of regret, realizing that he had disobeyed the instructions of his master.

Once they arrived at the temple, I secured the horse and cart and gently ushered both of them toward the room where we were to be taught. As we were entering, the Old Tibetan noticed that the young man was strangely unstable. Once the lesson began, he asked, 'Why do I feel that you are suicidal?'

As soon as this was mentioned, the man looked over at the disciple that brought him every day to the temple, who gasped, in apparent surprise. The Master realized immediately that the disciple had deviated from his instructions and thus interfered with the process of his teachings.

Before the two of them left at the end of that day, the devotee approached him briefly and said, 'Oh, Master, I gasped because I could feel that too.' The old Tibetan smiled and said in a gentle tone, 'Yes, indeed. We'll see you tomorrow at the same time.'

The next day what occurred was very unusual. My Master arose early and said to me, 'Turya, I have a feeling that the horse and cart may not arrive today. I don't know why I have become aware of this, but can you prepare the donkeys to go pick them up?'

I did as my Master had instructed, and, just as I was preparing to leave, they suddenly appeared from around the corner. The devotee immediately came to the Master to apologize. 'Sorry, I am a bit late,' he said, 'I thought I had damaged the wheel of the cart yesterday, but upon close examination I realized it is fine.'

The Old Tibetan said to him, 'I knew there was something wrong. I did not know why I asked Turya to prepare the two donkeys, but now I understand. Let's enter the sanctity of the temple to continue with our lessons.'

Time passed by harmoniously during their session, but the Old Tibetan noticed that the young man was deeply troubled by hidden feelings of suspicion. The Master realized that he had to reveal what he had seen.

Looking into his eyes, he said, 'You have brought something into the room which is of great importance. This will heal you and reveal why your timeline has been shifted and why I thought it was necessary to ask Turya to prepare our donkeys to go pick you up, even though there was seemingly no reason for this.'

Turning towards the older disciple, the Master said calmly, 'This is essential for all of us to learn from but especially for you, my devotee,' and then added, 'Turya, come sit by my side, it is important for you to witness this.'

The room was silent as the Old Tibetan began speaking.

'There is a phenomenon known as *discordant timeline convergence*. I will explain in great detail about this and how it affects the world around you so that you may communicate this in the future, if you feel it's necessary. Its manifestation is contingent on *Knowings and Doings*, but today we will focus on the results of actions that have an irreversible effect if not noticed.'

As the Master looked at his disciple, he said, 'Yesterday, when you gasped, and then told me that you had felt the suicidal tendencies of this young man, it was a lie to hide the fact that you had spoken about it the day before. I specifically asked you not to interfere with my teachings. Because you did not heed my warning, there are now many disruptive things happening simultaneously.

Firstly, when you were directing the horse and cart toward the village, you did not tell me that you thought the wheel was damaged. This affected my timeline via the fact that I went to Turya and asked him to prepare the two donkeys for a journey, though I did not know why.

It was only when you told me you thought there may

have been a problem with the cart that I realized what was behind this. This is how the *Unknown* speaks to one's heart.

I could have said that I knew why I was doing that, to make myself look wiser than what I am. But I did not. It is imperative, from the standpoint of our own progression, not to pretend we know anything more than what we know, for this becomes the lie which betrays the truth of what could truly be seen.

Now, the next thing that we must deal with is the suspicion within our guest toward me. When you lied about not interfering with him, you had no idea that I knew you were trying to deceive me.

Because he thought we were in cahoots with each other and that I was in possession of what you had discussed with him instead of what I had truly perceived, I decided to reveal what I knew to relieve him of his distrust.'

The disciple, at this point, raised his hands in the air and said, 'Master is telling the truth. I did not share with him what we had discussed.'

The young man looked at the Tibetan and said, 'I've never met anybody so aware. You knew I was suspicious. You knew your disciple had been dishonest. I am glad to have witnessed this and I know, because of what has happened, that I can trust you.'

The Master looked at his disciple and asked, 'Can you see now what your actions have produced? Still, there is much more. There are four ships in this room, travelling upon the ocean of our awarenesses. Each vessel was altered via your deception.

Consequently, I woke up early and instructed Turya to prepare the donkeys, not knowing why. Simultaneously, the visitor to our temple was full of suspicion, which was contorting his timeline. You were feeling guilt, and because of this you had added to your own cargo ship lies and manipulation.

This could have altered all of our destinies to such a degree that we may not have been able to recover. Can you see how complex this is? Can you all see that our destinies can be shifted through what seems to be insignificant yet has implications that are so far reaching?'

We were all silent as the clear and powerful voice of my Master lovingly held our attention in place.

'Within this delicate circumstance, communication is either true or false. I am being true to all of you in revealing how my timeline was altered via my disciple's dishonesty; how your suspicion of me was inflamed because of that; and how ultimately this room was rearranged in such a way that you could have left this precious occasion with doubt and mistrust instead of hope.'

Looking at his disciple he said softly, 'Your guilt blinded you for a split second, thus allowing the wheel of the cart to bump into a big rock. This made you think it could be damaged to such a degree that it would not be functional.

This was mixed in with feelings of regret and remorse, and that led you to believe in an exaggerated manner that the wheel could possibly be broken. Here we must realize that imbalanced feelings projected towards an inanimate object will return to the sender the horror that they have become.

Even though this rock does not seem to be aware, it obviously has reflective consciousness. Consider this.

Is this not simply your heart, revealing to you that you had deviated from my instructions and betrayed your own word? Did not the rock reflect that back to you? *Split the wood and lift the stone. You will find yourself there.* Do you see?

I knew that you had purposely misled me, but I waited to see what would occur because of your inability to follow this simple instruction.'

Reaching towards him and touching his knee, the Tibetan continued, 'It is important for you to understand that at no point am I attempting to guilt you for your mistake. I only want you to see that this missed opportunity is a test of the *Unknown*, which has revealed itself as an obstacle for you to overcome. This is all that is necessary to be realized.'

Listening attentively to the Mango Grove Master relaying this powerful story to them, one of the disciples wanted to know more. He said to the Sage, "Master, I am a little confused. The complexity of this situation is not completely clear within my mind. Could you please explain further?"

The Grove Master turned toward his disciple and patiently began to reiterate from another perspective what had taken place. "I suppose this could be difficult to understand. I believe it is very clear, but what I am expecting of you is to put together all the variables of the story in a way which is different to normal perception.

It was when these events occurred that I became very deeply aware of the destabilizing effects of *Knowings and Doings* and how they can bring about negative timeline convergences within our solid three-dimensional world. As you know, I've described this to you previously as the wooden spokes.

You see, the Old Tibetan knew that his disciple had been untrue to him but did not want him to feel shame. Simultaneously, the powerful man that was invited to the monastery had been triggered into suspicion towards the Master, thinking that the devotee had spoken and given him information.

The Old Tibetan knew this and needed to mend the torn fabric of the reality of that young man and relay to him the actual truths so that he could heal the wounds of dominance within him that were now appearing as mistrust."

The Mango Grove Master looked at his disciple to confirm that he had understood before continuing. "This is the *thief* and *ghost* that are normally transported between people who are untrue to one another.

The Tibetan was attempting to explain to all involved that this simple interaction of his disciple had altered the events of the day irreversibly—to the extent that he asked me to prepare the donkeys for a road trip. Realize, my friends, this was my Master's awareness being alerted to the fact that something was wrong.

Our consciousness is influenced via the wooden spokes, yet the holographic access point of that reality attempts to reveal the discord. Understand, there is one thing that truth relies upon, and that is open-hearted transparency.

My Master was in possession of fifty percent of the

information. His disciple, who had incorrectly intervened, was in possession of the other portion, and this became his feelings of guilt. The Tibetan knew he had lied, but he did not know about him running over a rock."

At this point, Master Turya looked up and said, "The Old Tibetan wanted to emphasize this one thing: The intuitive portion of his consciousness instructed his body to act in a way which was unusual because of the discordant feelings from somebody else that had played a part in the previous days' activities. In other words, he prepared the donkeys, not knowing why.

Here is where the Tibetan Master could be tested, yet there was no test to be had because he would not pretend that he knew something he didn't. Many false teachers, at this point, would proclaim, 'I prepared the donkeys because I knew you had damaged the cart.'

This is a very dangerous form of discordance. In reality, the other half of the truth was contained within the disciple. When the Master said, 'I only have half of the information,' he was honoring his truth. The other portion came to light when the disciple revealed he thought he had damaged the cart.

For the Tibetan Master, not knowing *why*, was not a test. It simply revealed that the jigsaw puzzle of his reality had humbleness at its core. So, when he said, 'I am in possession of only fifty percent of the information,' he was transmitting the voice of the *Unknown*, and this is a message that is very rarely heard.

No matter what you think you know, there is more to be realized. It is a test, and not a test, simultaneously. But if an individual lies, proclaiming to know more than what they do, then the puzzle—the fabric of that person's life—will be irreversibly changed. They will be chased by that deception within themselves.

The Old Tibetan was revealing, within that circumstance, the irreversible effects of a bias that does not want to be seen. These truly are the wooden spokes.

But remember, interwoven within all of this is the Old Tibetan's holographic perspective, which is determined upon his unwavering devotion towards the truth of his realizations to reveal the diverse implications that appear in between all interactions.

He was illustrating that there is no good or bad, right or wrong. There is only a very clear prospect in front of us all. It simply is as it is, without any feelings of bias either way. It is like when you climb the mountain. Should you feel offended if you accidentally slip into a ravine and break a leg? I think not.

Conversely, you could say, 'I fell but did not die. Something good is protecting me.' This is also not true. It is as it is.

Life will serve to show you that destiny provides you with a puzzle. Is it not imperative now to understand that there is no good, nor is there any bad? It is what it is. This reveals to all sentient *Beings* how to proceed without bias.

But if the corrupt try to hide their deception and the virtuous attempt to reveal the corruption, is this not a never-ending battle? For sure, it is.

If it is the way it is, the good will not have to fight, and the bad will not be compelled to hide. Nature simply gives us a choice via dualism, which are the wooden spokes attempting to show us that they truly do not exist.

All that matters is that we see what needs to occur. Not via our intervention but through the capacity of the laws of nature to reveal to us what is meant to happen next—so that we can incrementally awaken to the larger picture instead of looking at the world through a fisheye lens, from the viewpoint of our mind that irreversibly takes us away from our origin. The power of intuition cannot be sustained through lies.

Hopefully, now, my dear disciples, you can see with absolute clarity that power manifests in many different ways. It is of vital importance when communicating what arises in one's life that truth underpins all events. Only then will the true variables appear, and it is here that full recognition of our destiny is realized."

THE CHANT

"Now I would like to reveal to you an experience of my life to help establish a deeper understanding within your feeling center. This story perfectly illustrates the intricacies hiding within our moments, which is a crucial subject to review.

Remember, a power or a *siddhi* can be corrupted by one's bias *or* can be seen for exactly what it is—an impartial awakening of the *Unknown* towards one's devotion.

The reason why I am reminding you of this is that even if you are clear, when a power becomes available, your acknowledgement of it may become possessive, thus turning this phenomenon against you through your need to control and claim it as your uniqueness. This has to be avoided.

The movements that I have taught you will manifest powers within you that are only a byproduct of your awakening towards the love and tenderness that you will acquire within the process of ascension. Here, I believe there are only two choices, and this is precisely what I wish to speak with you about.

Let us begin to examine what has occurred in my life here in the Mango Grove. Within one's devotion, distinct sensitivities emerge. When somebody comes to visit, I am drawn towards their subtle frequencies, though I have no idea why.

There is a mysterious presence that arises from within, like a silk thread, imperceptibly pulling my light *Being* toward its destination. My body follows this directive, offering no resistance. I simply observe, for this is the *Not Doing* of that animation.

I have a dear friend who sometimes comes and visits. He loves to chant and when he does, the grove is full of the

THE CHANT

wonderful utterances of *Om Mani Padme Hum*. One day he was sitting under the Bodhi tree, totally absorbed in his practice, while I was tending to the orchard, transfixed by his chanting.

I noticed that my body was being unexpectedly led towards the path that surrounds the shed where our tools are stored. I had the feeling that there were three people there but wasn't quite sure whether it was so.

I followed this subtle intuition and made my way towards the shed. Turning the corner, I noticed that my gaze was beckoned to examine the wall, and, as I did so, a vortex appeared. I looked right through the surface. It was as if time and space stood still for a moment, and the neutrality of *No Place* opened up toward my *Being*. That's when I saw three men standing there, appearing like clear jelly, with light illuminating from within their physical form.

At that point, I recognized them as visitors from the village. I proceeded to walk to the back corner of the shed and looked around gently. The young men jumped, startled, and, upon seeing me, immediately bowed in reverence.

THE CHANT

'Oh Master,' they said, 'we did not want to disturb your friend, so we decided to sit here and listen to his melodic chant.' I smiled and invited them over, saying, 'Come, let's sit together under the Bodhi tree.'

Affectionate greetings were exchanged by all as we joined the others in the cool shade.

'Let us speak about the magic that has just occurred. It is a gift for all of us to witness. The culmination of your intentions that are filled with goodness and hope towards our enlightenment has set in motion an extraordinary event.

Your tender gratitude towards the chanting itself revealed the opening of a *nadi* within my *Being*—a silken thread that pulled upon an internal power, manifesting as a *siddhi*, which I believe is the coalescence of our combined awarenesses rising to the surface to be noticed.

The reason I say this is that it is a reflection of our hopes and dreams. Even though they have manifested as a power within me, I recognize this as the divinity of all involved. You will begin to see how this happens, once I explain what has occurred as a result of our collective devotion within the grove.

There are two potential outcomes of what just took place. The first is the most mundane aspect of such a power. The second is the *divine*, availing itself to be seen.

I have just been tested, and I would like to share with you all how a very subtle equilibrium allowed me to softly travel upon that silken thread and what I realized because of this.

As I walked towards the shed, I found I could see through the wall and clearly identify who was gently listening to my friend's chanting. The fabric of reality liquefied right before me as one of my internal *nadis* opened up.

Here, I was given a choice: to acknowledge that I had the power to see, or to understand that I am being seen. It is a very delicate affair. As you know, I am inclined to disregard my abilities, and that is for a good reason. Through that non-engagement, the *Unknown* becomes available by releasing oneself from the potential activation of a bias.

Within that circumstance the *divine emptiness* had opened up my three-dimensional reality, and, through this recognition, I had the fortune to understand that I was simultaneously being viewed.

At that moment, there were two frequencies availing themselves: One, to believe that I had discovered a power. Or, two, that power had provided a way to discover that I am being witnessed by the ethereal essence of that animation—the *Universal Beingness of No Place.*'

"My dear disciples, can you see the choice that was presented in that past circumstance? To be lost in my own need to be recognized or to realize that something beyond my reality is gently knocking on the doors of my perception to reveal that I am being observed.

I had no alternative but to choose the latter. As you know, power can imprison through desire, whereas our *Not Doings* may release us from this burden and allow us to continue upon our journey without the affliction of the need to be noticed."

The disciples were all listening attentively to what their Master was relaying when he suddenly asked, "Do you have any questions?"

"Master, when you speak about the silk thread being pulled within you by somebody else's presence and you follow that to see what it reveals to you, is what you notice contingent on the intention of that person?"

"Yes," replied the Old Sage, "but the thread that is being pulled within me is void of itself. It is so silent that my body follows it without knowing why. This is where one comes upon the *divine*. Only when you get closer to that momentary revelation, do you begin to realize what you know.

On this occasion it was extremely beautiful. I was transported by the chanting of my friend and simultaneously being pulled by the presence of our visitors. Realize, my body is a conduit, and I am merely a passenger that follows its inclinations.

This is the secret of secrets. The one who voyages within the physical form must reawaken to the implications of their journey within the subtleties of their neutrality being called upon."

"Master, when you looked through the wall and you saw the three men hidden behind it, what actually happened? How was information relayed to you in this extraordinary experience?"

"Firstly, I saw the men. I was looking toward them, but it was a world much different to the one you would expect. If I had any sense of grandeur within myself, I would declare: *I have seen*. But in reality, the *divine essence of No Place* was actually witnessing me through that porthole, beckoning my inner awareness to realize its subtle communion.

These are the tenuous threads that we begin to traverse. Once a person has conquered the entrapments of *Knowings and Doings*—and therefore their *Not Doings* are no longer encumbered by any form of self-reflective bias—their heart will be free to observe incoming communication."

"Master, you said you had the feeling that there were three people behind the shed, but you were not sure it was so. Was your feeling a *Knowing* at that point?"

"It was a gentle declaration of the *Beings* within the grove transmitting to me that there was something to be discovered. I am referring to the old mango trees. We not only have mycelia complex active within the root systems beneath us, this phenomenon of bio-energetic entanglement has evolved to travel upon the luminescence of the light filaments that surround us within the air as photons.

Realize that the stars above us communicate in the very same fashion. The way to confirm this for yourself is to lay upon the ground and gaze into the night sky. If you are patient, you will notice light fibers extending from one star to another. We have been surrounded by this luminous essence for billions of years. And now that you understand this, you will automatically be transported into the mystery of why you are here, in comparison to who you are.

We are all connected. It is just a question of whether we are awakened enough to realize it. Remember, though, you cannot rush towards that which is within you."

AS I AM

"Master, how is conquering one's self-reflective bias helping us truly know ourselves and also know others? Can you please speak more about this?"

"Let us all journey once again into Buddha's saying."

As I am, so are others; as others are, so am I. Having thus identified self and others, harm no one, nor have them harmed.

There are four parts to this scripture, yet I would ask you to realize there is a fifth, hidden meaning, that weaves through every part as either a *blessing* or a *curse*.

The first part is *As I am, so are others.* This can reference the dogmatic application of *Knowing and Doing*—its never-ending repetitive nature. As a human being, we have within us darkness and light. Yet take heed, when a flower faces the sun, though a shadow falls behind it, never once does it turn toward that directive. Its purpose in life is to know the *Doing* of the sun as an angelic light streaming towards its *Being*. The flower knows it is bathed within that luminescence.

The *Knowings and Doings* of the plant receive in humbleness that warmth and transport it deep within its tenderness. Here is where the sun becomes the *Not Doing* of the plant. There is no discord. This is a pure expression of *As I am, so are others*, and *As others are, so am I*, is its decree.

Now we can see that the sun and the delicate flower are one and the same. It is self-evident that, once we come upon the next verse, *Having thus identified self and others, the flower would not harm the sun, nor the sun harm that flower.*

This is the highest form of communion and the deepest gratitude that can ever be experienced. The *Knowings and Doings* are not harmful via the fact that neither of them is concerned with any outcome other than just *being their beautiful, loving selves.*

If I were to press a flower towards your cheek, would not the sun within you shine? Does not its angelic *Beingness* infuse within your humanness, effortlessly reflecting back that beauty?

Can you not see at this point that the highest form of communion surrounds us at every moment? This is what needs to be realized so that you may come upon the angelic song of the *Earth*, reaching through the petals of the flower toward the loving embrace of the sky which sends forth its luminosity in return.

Now we must revisit Buddha's saying once again, from a human perspective, in terms of the suffering that we all come upon via misunderstanding.

As I am, so are others; As others are, so am I is *Knowing and Doing, Doing* itself within its *Knowing*. This perpetual loop never reaches the next level of graduation, and, unfortunately, the final portion of the saying: *Having thus identified self and others, harm no one, nor have them harmed,* is not realized.

Each individual caught at this stage may understand only very limited information that pertains solely to *Knowings and Doings* within their repetitions. From this solidified viewpoint, a lowly heart will proclaim within its poverty, *As I am, so are others; as others are, so am I.* It is obvious that here, this represents perpetual suffering.

Yet, when this same impoverished heart evolves through much trial and tribulation, more love becomes available. Their light will begin to shine within, and they will say, *As I am, so are others,* with wholly different implications.

They will recognize the light in another person, drawing to themselves the inner *Being* of those they witness. *As others are, so am I.* Here is where one's heart discovers communion, faithfulness, love and tenderness, and, within that sacred exchange, abundance of truth.

As a collective, humanity progresses through many diverse circumstances. We will be reawakened ten thousand times, realizing within our humbling: *As I am, so are others.*

Knowing that peace and love reside within, we become empty of ourselves and begin *Not to Do* everything that is *Done*, thus coming upon the first mystery of *No Place.*

Understanding *As others are, so am I,* and being so completely devoid of self, we begin to recognize the variances within a person's feelings that enter us to be witnessed. And so, unbeknown to ourselves, we herald the truths of another's voice within us.

Now we have graduated the first part of Buddha's saying and we arrive upon the second verse, only to realize that we are back at the beginning again: *As I am, so are others; as others are, so am I.*

Not only have we overcome the obstacles of perception that challenged our tenderness, but through diligently *Not Doing*, we begin to come upon unity as a whole. This is when certain truths become self-evident.

Having thus identified self and others, harm no one, nor have them harmed, is the prospect of our collective future.

There are wheels within wheels hidden in this Buddhist scripture. Can you identify where you are right now?

As I am, so are others.

I have shown you the *blessing*. Can you see the *curse*? The wooden spokes of our timelines at this present juncture in history are colliding, with devastating ramifications.

As I am, so are others can be a wooden spoke—a curse—or a holographic song, an angelic embrace that reveals its magic to disentangle one's bindings. By peeling back the layers within Buddha's saying, many blessings are arrived upon.

For those of you who have ears to hear, be awakened to the light within you. *No Place* is full of the most *divine* proclamations. Love and understanding is all that matters."

"Master, could you explain in more detail about hard and soft collisions? Is this the same as the difference between the wooden spokes and the holographic aspect of the wheels?"

"The wooden spokes have a quality of being solidified.

There is an enormous amount of pressure that surrounds their collisions. Their rigidity only perceives what they encounter as resistance, which manifests as overt or unseen forms of conflict.

In other words, the inner eye of the individual recognizes duality as their dominion and fights for the wrong outcome because of their preoccupation with identifying what they think needs to be done. There is an emphasis on thinking here.

This is why I described the internal dialogue to be similar to a stubborn donkey that will not budge from its position no matter how much you plead for it to move.

The holographic wheels are represented as holograms that are vacuous within their composition. They have the capacity to pass through each other, acknowledging the essence of what is being observed from a deeply introspective viewpoint, and automatically adapting to the laws that are the inherent nature of our universe.

They are wholly animated within their reflection of

emptiness, harmoniously turning with respect to all circumstantial variables. They can be seen as having eyes on all surfaces that acknowledge everything encountered. This encompassing awareness is what we are all evolving toward as a humanity. Everything that one individual notices is absorbed by every other *Being*, instantly. It is a form of harmonious entanglement.

"Can you explain in more depth what obstacles represent? How does this relate to the 'cobblestones' of one's life?"

"Imagine that you have taken ten thousand steps, which is a monumental feat, and, on your journey toward the sublime, a person calls upon you to notice them. By turning around and proceeding towards the way they have beckoned, you land upon their path. At this point you realize that they have only taken approximately five hundred steps within their life.

You look around to observe your own path and see that you are faced with a very strange challenge. Your ten thousand steps at this point have been reduced to the scope of five hundred. We will call this what it truly is—an obstacle.

As you communicate, you realize who you are encountering within the limitations presented, but you do not call upon judgment within yourself. This will overcome your first dilemma. It is a discipline which will define you, *even though it cannot be seen by anybody but you*. You have taken ten thousand steps, and you know you remain invisible to the perspective of five hundred.

This is your next obstacle to overcome. Only you will know what occurs within you. If your devotion is applied incorrectly to that circumstance with that individual, this in itself will change you. You must fully live your truths even though you cannot be seen. When you realize how to apply yourself in a way that does not compromise your heart, you will see that the destiny of the person who you are observing is restricted via their perception.

If you notice that they are missing an opportunity to be themselves—knowing that they have no way of seeing you—and if, at that moment, you do not judge them, something extraordinary will occur.

You will see the path they were meant to take, and the beauty of their cobblestones will be revealed—even if they are acting in a way which is contrary to the potential you have recognized. Witnessing this will bring forth your compassion, to relieve you of the burden of what you have noticed."

"Master, you have mentioned *qualities*, in the past. Could you speak about what a *quality* is?"

"Within all my years of diligently practicing, I have noticed within my biofield a particular feeling that was very strong in the early stages of my journey and which has increased over time. Sometimes when I stand up, I feel a massive weight surrounding my body. This quality is a sensation of gravity that all other subtle phenomena will adhere to. Even though I am speaking about myself, it is instructional for you as well.

Everyone can access a certain predominant feeling that is their quality in the beginning. This sensation is the first clue your body gives you towards your progress. I don't want you to misunderstand or underestimate what I am saying now. It is something that took me years to fully realize.

Imagine this: You are sitting on a chair and you slowly bend your body forward. You will begin to sense that something is weighing upon your upper torso. It will be very heavy, but if you move quickly to an upright position you will lose it.

The most profound secret within the system that I have taught you is that you must cultivate that initial quality of gravity and not lose that feeling when transitioning to another resonance that is attempting to calibrate your *Being*.

Eventually all elements synchronize. The entirety of the feelings will homogenize as a collective frequency, and you won't notice that there are four to eight qualities harmonizing as one. This is mastery. It will be true to you if you are true to it."

THE BLESSING

Master Turya sensed that his disciples and the visitors to the grove had many questions. With a nod and an encouraging glance, he urged them to begin.

"Master, how do we shift other people's timelines via our *Not Doing* them?"

"We do not really shift them. We reduce our influence upon them. By *Not Doing* somebody, you withdraw the burden of bias that is contingent upon your *Doings*. It is important to realize that our missed opportunities are presently available upon our moment that is continuously escaping us. *The past is right in front of you!*

Forgive the other person for who they were and within this revelation, come upon who you are, in comparison to what you are witnessing. *Know* what you've seen is true to a certain degree; then, with love and understanding, withdraw until you arrive upon the unexpected."

"Master, is *Being, Knowing, and Not Doing* somebody, and *Being, Knowing, and Not Doing* oneself part of being a *Passerby*?"

"Yes, it is. Applying the *Passerby* principle requires you to be absolutely openhearted within your yielding. The only way to embrace yourself is to release somebody else from your *Knowings and Doings* of them."

"Master, what is it inside of us that makes us focus upon the wrong things in other people?"

"See it this way. If what is noticed can be recognized as a lost opportunity, this will lead you to discover the sacredness within that reckoning. Acknowledging when one has made a mistake allows one to be humbled."

"Master, I often grapple with feelings transferred to me

with harmful intent and struggle to put discordant projections to hard work. How can I deal with this?"

"You must put these things into labor or love. Forgive the other person and remember that the obstacle that was put in front of you is nothing but a test that will show you exactly who you are. Be constantly vigilant to the *ghost* and the *thief,* and do not allow them to reinitiate themselves within you. Is this not your challenge to reflect upon? Your next task is to forgive yourself.

Forgiveness and hard work are not only a tender kiss upon somebody else's cheek, but also a means for learning to turn this loving embrace towards yourself. You are the commander of your vessel and you beat within your own chest. Don't you?"

"Master, what should I do if I realize that I am the sour fruit and have betrayed myself and everybody else?"

"Come upon your own sweetness. Don't *Do* 'you' anymore. By learning to inwardly reflect, sourness will be turned into regret. And, if you don't shame, blame, or guilt yourself, a revelation will open your heart to be revealed to you. Here you will enter the end of your life, metaphorically speaking, no matter what age you are.

It's simple—just withdraw from who you were. Be kind and loving until you disappear. You are only being tested by your own obstacles."

"Master, how do you find the neutral place of yourself, your inner *Being*, when the mind won't stop in terms of the feelings that it's creating?"

"You are creating your feelings. You are in command of your mind. *Be responsible for your emotions.* Stand up now and go to the field. Pick up a handful of fertile soil, draw it to your face and smell how wonderful it is. Then turn to the sun and feel it caressing your skin. Will this not change you?"

"Master Turya, how do you cope with being between your human existence and *No Place*, and why did this happen to you?"

"Let's talk about you instead of me. If you can be full of devotion and love in a world which at times may seem to be harsh, this will train you to *Not Do* you—until you disappear. Love the people who love you. Accept the people who don't like you, and realize that a field of flowers is appreciated even more after walking upon dry, barren land."

"Master, you've spoken about powers that are *siddhis* that appear in response to the opening of *nadis* in your body. Some of those you have consciously disregarded, but you have also integrated many of them. Can you describe what they are?"

"I feel grateful. I am honored that many people love me. What arises from within my chest is more important than what I can create with my hands. Does not the pottery of my creation reveal a different shape in every circumstance that is me? Is not my container empty, yet permanently full? This is my secret."

"Master, you said that we are suspended between *Heaven and Earth*. I have become more physically powerful recently, and what I want to know is: How do I circulate and balance the sexual energy in my body as I become stronger?"

"Chop wood and carry water. Put that abundance to work as purpose and service. The power of your primal energy will naturally transform itself within your lower gourd. This will, in turn, bathe your heart in joy, filling your internal eye with light. Then, you will realize that love and understanding is all that matters."

"Master, you have hinted many times that you have had experiences with interstellar *Beings*. Can you talk a little about this?"

"Everything that I teach you right now, and everything I have ever mentioned, resounds with their feelings. I am attempting to show you how to come upon this attunement within yourself, thus beckoning them to return our loving intention sent. Love and devotion seeks love and devotion, eternally."

"Master, in all the years that we've known you, we have noticed that you have disappeared on many occasions, sometimes for days. Why do you do this?"

"If a riverbed is barren and dry, how can it possibly

quench your thirst? This is why I retreat: to replenish my resources so that I may have the capacity to be more than I am. The years have taught me that we must be full of energy and flowing with abundance—clear and strong, yet reflective. It is important for us to realize when we are riverbed-dry."

"Master, we know that you are a highly-skilled martial artist. Why don't you want to fight anymore? And why don't you want to teach this?"

"I once was who I used to be. Now I am who I was meant to become. If you come upon a field of light, do you need to raise your fist?

"Master, how does your body feel when someone is disloyal to you? And how do you know what they are going to do before they do it?"

"Even those who oppose us call us to observe them. An obstacle is a burden, this is true. But the true burden is not to be aware that you are involved in the obstacle."

"Master, you told us there are many different types of timeline convergences, even within only one lifetime. Can you speak about that?"

"Everybody we meet becomes an intersection. We are subtly moved by this contact. Doesn't one ship passing within the oceans of your life create ripples upon the waters of your realizations? Don't these fluctuations beckon your eyes to look within yourself to discover their origin? We have thousands upon thousands of opportunities that allow us to grow."

"Master, how is the relationship between a man and a woman really supposed to be? What keeps a couple together?"

"The simple answer is: *Love and Devotion*. And devotion to that love. That's what keeps us all together."

"Master, how do we return to sincerity if its delicate frequency has been disturbed by a collision with the wooden spokes?"

"Forgive the one who has transgressed upon your tenderness, even when *you* are that person. Entering the light is sometimes difficult. That is why it is so very important to realize that the reflection within the water is you."

"Master, why is it that one becomes more aware of their hallways of light upon being confronted with subtle disharmony?"

"The only way to realize your resources is to have them tested."

"Master, you were saying: *The heart in actuality is the original progenitor of our intelligence.* Can you speak about the role of intellect from this perspective?"

"There is no intellect to be spoken of once one realizes the voice of their heart."

"Master, you said you have experienced two types of white light. Can you talk about that?"

"There are many variations within frequency. One attunement may attract another. Our experiences are contingent upon these variances. It is hard for me to explain what I have seen or why. It would be even more difficult for me to say to you what I believe you are going to come upon.

Do you understand my answer? If not, then at least you

may comprehend your own question more deeply."

"Master, you mentioned you have had contact with Yeshua. Could you tell us more?"

"Is not your heart beating within your chest right now? Will you not travel upon the timeline that is your destiny and arrive upon who you are, in comparison to who you were?"

"Master, in my meditation, I have come upon a quietude that is hard to describe, other than to say it feels like my *simple self*, emerging. It is from this emptiness that I so wish to live. However, in the distractions and interactions of daily life, I soon fall back into believing my thoughts, succumbing to the *thief*, repeating old patterns of behavior—and all too often I find myself once again stuck, in a dark place, unsure of how to proceed.

How does one best go beyond this negativity that usurps our sovereignty? How does one take that leap, which leads towards our right to happiness, attunement, or even ascension?"

"Firstly, be careful not to assume anything. Let life come

upon you. There is no right, nor wrong.

If you believe you have gained your quietude, your silence, yet continue to affirm your obstacles, you may be becoming lost within a form of self-aggrandizement. Obstacles will always be there. So will the quietude. Seize upon neither one of them. The question is: Are you caught within your own duality right now?

When you enter a room, if a door is closed, don't you reach for a handle to leave that space and enter another chamber? And if you discover that the next environment is disharmonious, is it not pertinent to move on?

Furthermore, if your silence is an escape from that which you are meant to face, is that stillness true to you?

Obstacles are a rite of passage. Face them and be what is required of you. Then your quietude will arise to be witnessed. To know the left, you must embrace the right. To know the right is to embrace the left. To step forward does not necessarily mean you leave something behind."

"Master, I understand that we have the option to see

memories characterized by negativity as missed opportunities. When you say we can *transform the discordant past and thereby become who we could have been*, how, exactly, is this accomplished?

Are we meant to reconstruct the past event and re-envision it differently? Is this something we need to do in our imagination when a memory arises wreathed in negativity and one feels guilt, self-recrimination, or blame? Or, instead, do we need to let it go—to *Not Do* that memory by releasing it completely?"

"*Be your simple, beautiful self.* This is all that is required of you. To look back is to realize an opportunity has been missed. To be yourself *right now* is to take that misfortune and turn it into a blessing. You are no longer that curse. Know this. Ponder upon it deeply.

Am I a *blessing* or am I a *curse?*

This is all you need to ask. These two words are very powerful. A curse is an obstacle. A blessing is to see through it and realize that the affliction has caused you to turn and face that disharmony. Our redemption is to recognize the radiance of the sun upon our entire *Being*. Once again, *are we not like flowers bathing within the light?"*

"Master Turya, when you mentioned to sustain a stance of non-interference, are you referring to our thoughts as well as actions? How shall we employ this delicate art in relation to being in service to others? And how do we differentiate whether a minor interference on our part is also applying a form of *Knowing and Doing?"*

"Be aware of your micro-gestures. Take responsibility for your intent. Don't fall victim to yourself in terms of negativity. Like an innocent child, be open. Yet, at the same time, allow the wings of your fortune to lift you high into the sky where no man's feelings can reach. Imagine you have climbed to the top of a mountain. Are you affected by someone in the valley, gently walking upon their journey?"

"Master, sometimes when I am deep within my practice, the contours of my life—as a residual image of self—dissipate entirely. All the occurrences that once seemed so real, or stories which have happened, are nowhere to be found. Are memories similar to the *ghost* and *thief* you were telling us about earlier, but in a larger context? And would it be true to say that they never existed in the first place?"

"You have just answered your own question. Remember that the *thief* and the *ghost* are a human construction that feeds on dualism. Once a person begins to *Not Do* themselves, they will naturally come upon quietude and sacredness.

Whatever appears beyond this point is not an ongoing manifestation in terms of repetitious memory, but the beginning of beginnings, as far as consciousness is concerned. Withdrawing the past imagery that you have described from the vastness will lead you back home to the tenderness of that which has generously, with absolute devotion, followed everything you have ever done.

You are its outward expression. When you realize that the emptiness's response to you is *Not to Do* you, you will be pulled closer to it. Here is where you will return to the source."

"Master, you once mentioned something about graduating via forms of forgiveness:

Thus, we dissolve our Knowing and enter into one of the first forms of forgiveness so that we can graduate this dissonant frequency as an act of devotion.

Is there a second form?"

"Of course. Forgiving someone's *Knowings and Doings* is a first step towards devotion to that person. When transporting this feeling back into the body, it is then graduated into a *Not Doing* of yourself, and that person, simultaneously.

The frequency that arises from this dedication becomes an upward ascension—an awakening of one's heart toward all *Beings*. Here is another point of graduation.

We step back gradually into our light. Then, and only then, will the ever-present, unknown quality of our emptiness step forward to engulf us. When this occurs, we begin to realize that our time has ended. Yet we continue embracing life and being embraced by the source. Love and devotion is all that matters."

"Master, can you speak more about the white light? Must we always seek it?"

"No, you should not seek anything. You must allow it to come upon you. The only thing to take into consideration is the way you live your life. Becoming aware of the intricacies within your circumstances will assign your heart to all that can be noticed. This will help you become humble, revealing who you are, within your limitations. Is this not a gift?

If sunlight upon your face brings comfort, just be grateful. You did not beckon it to be there. You discovered it because it manifested before you. In this way, the world calls us. If a soft breeze gently caresses your clothing, are you not surrounded? Did it not seek you out because you were not seeking it? There is no way for you to pre-empt what you are meant to come upon.

When you walk upon the ground, does not the grass feel beautiful? When you then enter a field, isn't it natural to take refuge under an old tree? Were you drawn to it? The *Earth* avails its softness, offering comfort and solace. You did not desire these things, yet you began to commune with them, in answer to their call.

You cannot seek what is, but you certainly can be aware if something notices that you have noticed it. Our paths are very simple when we follow these truths, and within that simplicity, gratitude and love arises. Is this not a blessing?"

"Master, are we to seek correct motive or be without motive? Is there a difference? If so, what is it?"

"Have I not just answered that question? To have motive is a very subtle form of corruption. Remember, whatever you seek will echo back to you as your own wish to be rewarded. And doesn't expectation give you a feeling of entitlement that possesses you, because of your need to possess what you desire? This is the curse.

If you consider my answer to the previous question, you must ask yourself: Why did you not notice what I described as a blessing? And why is it that you pursued your inquiry in the way that you have?

THE BLESSING

The *thief* and the *ghost* are extremely complex in terms of what they propel you towards. If you were to worship an object on an altar, what are you really praying to? Why does that image draw you to it? Is it the design of your motive to seek out whatever power you can encompass within the parameters of your own fixation?

Perhaps the momentum of the collective intentions of many to worship that object, because of what they have heard the benefits may be, has baited your desire. Ask yourself if what you believe is your destiny comes down to your need to control the outcome of the world around you via the fact that you wish to be noticed.

When following the path of your ambition for too long, do you forget to feel the sun upon your face? And do you recognize the gentle fingers of the wind tugging on your garments, beckoning you to realize that you are surrounded by the *divine*?

Was it you who put a fence around the field and guarded the gate so that people may pay you to sit beneath the branches of a tree? Is this not the beginning of the end of all blessings? And do you not interfere with the call that beckons all *Beings* to enjoy its nourishing shade?

By creating the obstacle of payment to reach this beauty, does this not cause its blessings to become your curse upon the people who seek what is already there to be given?

To enter the ultimate threshold, one must be composed of light. For this to even begin to occur, one's tenderness, kindness, and understanding toward another human being must be completely free of the expectation of return. Here, one will start to realize that the call of the *divine* can only be sought through giving, not taking. This is truly a blessing.

As you sit here under the Bodhi tree, see that my disciples seek nothing of me, yet a call of their own heart allows them to recognize their teacher, thus opening the doorway for us to see one another. Via this simple communion, I have access to that which you cannot find. Seek not to see, nor hear; then what comes upon you will be felt and known.

Use your eyes, your ears, and your feeling in a way that

harbors no expectation. Through your *Inaction*, you will begin to understand. Upon this revelation, the *divine* will arise within your voice to show you where it truly resides. This is what we are all travelling toward."

"Master, is it possible for you to speak more about the elusive equilibrium that can be felt, fluctuating throughout our life? Does this delicate phenomenon have awareness of its own?

"The answer to your question is in a field of flowers, and within the gentle mist surrounding you in the rainforest. When you hear the crickets call, are they not accompanying the birds within the neighboring trees? Do you become aware of this, simply by *Being*?

Isn't your environment beckoning you to notice? To come upon the radiance within the complex world around you, you must seek your own luminosity within. Step back from what you know to discover the delicate equilibrium you seek.

When the upward-travelling fountain of your heart is

activated, you will begin to gain awareness of your internal hallways. Then, if you are diligent enough to withdraw, what surrounds you will reveal itself eventually.

Seeking out your own origin, you will discover the source of the animated light which appears as the manifest world. Be a blessing unto yourself.

"Master, when you spoke about *nadis* and *chakras*, you associated them with stars in the sky. Can you please say more about this network that lies deep within one's physical framework and differentiate between the seventy-two thousand *nadis*, the one hundred and fourteen smaller *chakras*, the seven major ones, and the internal hallways that you told us about?

What do they look like and what is their purpose? Is this configuration something which depends on the physical body? And what is the relationship between one's predisposition and the way this network organizes itself according to that?"

"Basically, when you ask these questions, the only way

that I can answer is to inform you how I have observed them. Firstly, the seven major *chakras* may be familiar to a lot of people as a concept, but, within their interdependent connectivity they are as complex as the whole network.

The way these seven *chakras* have appeared to me may be different to what you have studied. They oscillate independently within your body like discs or plates that can be activated to rotate like a spinning coin that is finding rest upon a table. To give an example, I have seen the *Manipura chakra* literally rotating under my skin, lifting the tissues in the solar plexus region, as if a disc were twirling in slow-motion.

The formless becomes manifest, enabling one within their journey to go from the level of the energy body to the physical, which may appear as movement initiated by the *chakra* itself. However, this is not a general rule of thumb. The visual description of this experience is to allow you to realize that the physical body and the *chakras* harmonize at certain points throughout your life, and for everyone this awakening will be different.

THE BLESSING

Even though I describe my path, you cannot walk upon it. You have to understand yours to realize mine. Regardless of the fact that I am giving you a true depiction, you will be within your own interpretation of what this really means. From a linear perspective, it can never be comprehended. It would just seem like magic.

To reiterate, attempting to pursue or replicate that which I have acquired over my lifetime is not what I am prescribing for you. This *chakra* intervened on my behalf as if it were independent from my consciousness. In other words, this is not a skill.

Seeing it physically manifest is different to perceiving it energetically. A *chakra* appears like a flower—each petal has a quality, and whichever way it is oscillating will reveal sensations that belong to the elemental structure of its form. In this case my physicality and the energy body were being activated via somebody else's intention. That answers your question without answering it. It is just the way it is.

I have only touched upon one description of the seven *chakras* here, and, unfortunately, it will remain abstract for there is no way to formulate concreteness within the question you have posed. To go into the complexities of what I realized regarding why it was moving as it did, might mislead you.

Each explanation which defines a center of energy can become a perceptual trap for those who want to emulate what is being described. Know this: *It is not possible.* You simply cannot measure your experiences upon somebody else's journey. But upon the cobblestones of your life you can certainly apprehend what was not understood previously, within your own awakening.

The other one hundred and fourteen *chakras* are smaller and obviously more diverse within the system. They also appear like flowers when they spin. There are hundreds of thousands, even millions of possibilities that can arise from their interconnectivity. But this is not about mathematics; it is a metaphor for a causality chain that wakes up upon itself within the human form.

Once again, this portrayal won't really help since there are so many factors to take into consideration which the rational mind will under no circumstances comprehend.

There are pathways that *nadis* and *chakras* travel upon. They are similar to small clusters of light that look like grapes hanging from a vine, yet do not really appear this way at all. They project threads from their spinning center to a new location within the inter-related mechanisms of light. This occurs between all the *chakras* traveling upon the complex pathways of one's animated consciousness.

Look at it this way, the system within the body of a person who has been conditioned or influenced to be what they are not meant to be is in actuality their perfect storm, and this is what I become aware of as a teacher. But, as you know, the storm is nowhere near perfection. It is just a repetitive causality chain whose limited variables are nevertheless so diverse that they cannot really be taken into rational consideration.

A socially-engineered individual, through being aligned by their circumstances, becomes harmonized within their suffering. This is *As I am, so are others* in the midst of its profound confusion.

THE BLESSING

What I am attempting to transmit to all that come in contact with me is that when your personality develops, it frames a pathway. This, in essence, is what one would call your destiny. You are in a state of determinism that has a causality highway within it that is habitually self-replicating. This is where the explanation has to end because it cannot go further than this.

The only way to fully—yet in an incomplete way—depict how this comprehensive energetic system impresses itself upon us is to relay to you in a very simple manner how situational awareness becomes attunement.

Through *Not Doing* we can release deterministic causality into its true nature—or free will—so that individuals can differentiate between who they are and who they could really be within their journey in this sacred vessel called the human body.

Now I would like to shift the focus from *that* to *this*. But remember: *That* is not *this* and *this* is not *that*. Unfortunately, though, it is the only way to comprehend the incomprehensible.

THE BLESSING

When I point my finger toward the moon, or if you see its reflection within a body of water, which image is real? If you say the moon within the sky, you show me where you are. Or do you see the reflection in the water as more real than the moon in the heavens? What is the truth if you have never been here on this planet before?

Once you live in this reality for a certain period of time you will be convinced when you say: *The moon is in the sky, not in the water, that is only a reflection.* But is that really true? Is up really up? Is down really down? Is North actually North when your compass says it is so?

If I would take you halfway between the moon and the earth and ask you: *Where is up and where is down, where is left and where is right?* Where is North at that point? You can say: *The moon is to my right; the earth is to my left.* This is true, but where is up and where is down? Does it really exist if the gravitational experience is not there anymore?

There is an abyss above you and an eternity below you. Our existence relies upon the physical representation of where we are. But are we really there?

THE BLESSING

If I move forward in between the earth and the moon is that really forward? Is behind really behind me? The sun and the moon are to my left and right, but does front and back really exist? What if I took away my physical representation in this visualization? Where am I now?

I would ask you to come back to the planet with me. If you feel confused at this point, you should. These are the obstacles I am challenging you to face; no mention of *nadis* or *chakras* here. What have you realized? Something about nothing, or nothing about something?

I will invite you to take a journey. Inside our bodies we have a perfect storm occurring within a network of light that is internally revealed. It moves like a hurricane along our pathways. The more we *Don't Do*, the more it *Does* us on the level of energy. It looks like a confluence of white filaments in a complex fusion that is ever-changing and magnificent to witness.

Within the appearance of that light, I see all possibilities becoming available via the innumerable opportunities that present themselves—but at the point of witnessing I am the outline of my physical form, contained within the radiance of the antenna that is my skin. Our perfect storm is complex. It is a wonder of wonders to observe. Eternity somehow compresses itself within a small beacon of light.

See it like this: Look into the night sky. Can you imagine all possibilities of points of communication in reference to the combinations of stars that you can actually see? What will occur if we relinquish the boundary that is the radiance that holds this perfect storm within our skin?

Now, let me ask you the simplest thing which, in reality, is so complex: How does one read people because of this? When one comes upon the disharmony that may have been spotted in the micro-gestures within someone's physical form, what is actually being seen is their perfect storm of imperfection within the labyrinth of one's system of light. This is how an empath sees.

Once noticing the network of complexity within the person being observed, my body realizes what they are *Doing* —which I *Don't Do*. This is all that matters, for all who are wondering what I am describing.

Am I not the reflection? Yet see it for what it really is—an illusion. This is how I detect where people are in comparison with my own complexities. You must navigate this within the parameters of your own imperfection, for within this we are all perfect. Here is where we come upon our humbleness.

I am only a point within the middle of the abyss, sending back my echo so that you may follow in my footsteps. Love eternally beckons itself to realize a more encompassing horizon. From whichever position you may find yourself in, there will you also find me.

GRATITUDE

"Master, you once mentioned something about honoring gifts. Can you tell us what you meant by that?"

"This is a very important subject. It is at the core of devotion. When someone gives me a gift, I don't receive it as merely the offering itself. It is acknowledged as if the person is there before me. Even after they have gone, it will be treated with reverence and a certain amount of due diligence.

I assign my attention to it, and as it is cared for, what is sent to that person is my feeling of love and devotion. Gifts are sacred. And the one who made that offering is precious as well.

GRATITUDE

If the gesture contains motive, that will be revealed. If it is made with tender care, without the need of return, that person will receive love and devotion. An act of generosity within itself is *divine*.

I know that someone's life can be transformed by treating the object of affection with love and care. I am contained within the feeling of these beautiful gestures. Our world is soft and tender. We just have to realize it."

"Master, how do we honor our ancestors?"

"When you respect someone, are you not paying homage to everything that has ever been enacted, in that very moment of communion?

When a mango tree passes you its fruit, isn't that your grandmother filling you with sweetness? Are not the bones of all our ancestors beneath our feet? When you kiss someone on their cheek, aren't you kissing the dust in their veins?

When you see a bird gliding upon the wind, isn't that your grandfather underneath its wings? When the stream flows down from the mountain, doesn't the water you drink contain the memories of every *Being* that has ever existed?

When we breathe the air that surrounds us, aren't we inhaling the breath of all those that have ever stood upon this planet? And when we exhale, haven't we joined them?

When you skin your knee and apply a plant medicine to your wound, did it not call upon you to find it? Isn't the planet of service to us? Does it not care for our well-being by becoming conscious of what we need?

This is the voice of our ancestors reaching into our vulnerability, saying, *I love you. I have never abandoned you and never will.*

When you begin to look at what you can't see, listen to what you can't hear, and come upon what cannot be touched, is this not the subtlest of subtleties allowing you to realize that the eternal, ever-present moment, composed of everything that has ever been done and forgotten, is now remembered within your momentary capacity to know?

If you can reach this most delicate state of consciousness, will you then realize your brothers and sisters that abide in other planetary systems are sending us their love through their trials and tribulations? Can you arrive upon the wisdom of their discernment through the refined emanation of their hearts beating toward us?

Who is looking at you when your eyes come upon something? That is the question.

Love unconditionally, because whether you realize it or not, love calls upon you in every moment that exists. Is it not love that we are searching for? Isn't this all that matters?

We are nothing more than an egg in a nest. Like the dove that broods devotedly toward its own offspring, our heart coos, sending forth a feeling of comfort so that we may arise within that embrace to sing beautifully the most tender reflection of who we are meant to be.

GRATITUDE

*Whatever you gaze at gazes back at you.
Within this exchange you will always find yourself inwardly reflected. This is your heart of hearts, calling and responding to itself. When you listen to the song of a beautiful bird, when you truly listen,
do you not hear yourself singing?*

For those of you who have ears to hear:

Now, can you see?

In gratitude for all of you who have read these pages,

I am humbled.

Lujan Matus

Can you walk

without your mind?

For information regarding workshops
and private tuition with Lujan Matus please visit:

www.parallelperception.com

Printed in Great Britain
by Amazon